'Here, in modern, sly, beautiful English, is the darkness of Chaos, the emergence of gods, the sunny glades of Pan and the creation of bewildered, finite man. It is lovely, sad, erotic and terrifying by turns. A continuous novel of quite extraordinary power'

— *Daily Mail*

'Rich, poetic, continually surprising with the original and exciting word or phrase, so that one experiences in detail this archetypal world. It will fire the imaginations of people of any age'

— *The Times Educational Supplement*

'Bursting at the seams with talent and imaginative energy, its blazing vitality and unquestionable coherence will make it appeal to many children who haven't warmed to these stories in more orthodox versions'

— *The Guardian*

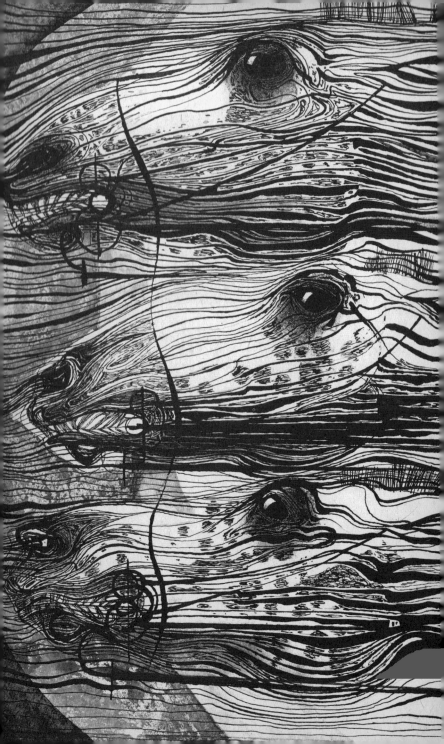

The God Beneath the Sea

Leon Garfield
and
Edward Blishen

Illustrated by Charles Keeping

CORGI BOOKS
A DIVISION OF TRANSWORLD PUBLISHERS LTD
A NATIONAL GENERAL COMPANY

THE GOD BENEATH THE SEA

A CORGI BOOK 0 552 09158 8

Originally published in Great Britain
by Longman Group Limited London

PRINTING HISTORY

Longman Group edition published 1970
Corgi edition published 1973

Corgi Books are published by Transworld Publishers Ltd,
Cavendish House, 57–59 Uxbridge Road, Ealing, London W.5

Printed in Great Britain by
Fletcher & Son Ltd, Norwich

Contents

To
Vivien,
Nancy
and
Renate

PART I

•

THE MAKING
OF THE GODS

1 ● The Seeds of Power

At first it was a tiny prick of light—as if the sun had gone too close and caught the immense blue fabric of the sky. It glinted and glittered and presently it was seen to be moving, like a golden needle stitching away at the heavens.

This was in the early morning. By noon its brightness had dimmed. Against the sun's full blaze it was no more than a charred and flaming mote. The sun continued toward the west; the sky deepened and the mote had increased till it was the size of a thumbnail held at full stretch.

Already its light cast a great pool of gold on the darkening sea and a curious sound was in the air. A thin wailing that rose at times to a scream. . . .

Now the sun was gone and the twisting, flickering, shining thing lit up a patch of the night as it rushed down to meet itself in the sea.

The sound grew shriller, louder. The waves began to tremble and hasten hither and thither in a panic. It was coming. . . . Then, for the briefest instant, the falling shape was seen quite clearly as it turned over and over in the air. It was a fiery, shrieking baby. . . .

Suddenly two white arms rose up out of the sea. They caught the infant as it fell and drew it swiftly down under the wave. The light was quenched and the sea rolled on, dark and peaceful under the stars.

The gaping fish and the blundering turtles fled away; the ornamental sea-horses and giant crabs that seemed to carry spired and blushing cities on their backs drifted and clambered into nooks and crevices as the goddess sped down among them in a pearly storm of bubbles.

Deeper and deeper she rushed with the frantic infant in her

arms. The formidable monsters on the ocean's floor curled and rolled away among the coral forests where the flash and glimmer of sea-nymphs lit the goddess on her way. At last she came to the entrance of a cave. Here, strange and intricate configurations of the rock caused the currents to twist and eddy and force the waters through a mighty conch shell so that they foamed and tumbled across the cave's threshold like the fleece of the sea-god's sheep.

The goddess paused, then stepped across the waters into the cave and the grotto beyond.

'Sister,' she murmured. 'Sister, here is the babe who fell from the sky.'

The two goddesses, Thetis and Eurynome, gazed down on the infant who had lapsed into a frowning sleep. For a long while they regarded its limbs and crumpled face. Neither spoke and the only sound in the grotto was the wild music the sea made as it rushed through the great conch that guarded the entrance to the cave. Then Eurynome said softly, 'Sister, though you did well to save him, there's no doubt he is . . . hideous.'

Thetis sighed. 'Yet he shone so brightly as he fell—'

'Then let us call him Hephaestus, the shining one, and—and hope he will improve.'

'Hephaestus,' whispered Thetis, bending so low over the sleeping child that her gleaming hair danced across his cheek. 'What kind of a god will you be?'

He slept in a silver cradle, and the mighty goddesses brought him such toys as became a baby—rattles of coral and pearls, glittering pebbles and curious shells. They fashioned a crystal window in the rock so he might watch the uncanny world that glimmered away into a green eternity. Sometimes the sea-nymphs would come to this window and press their faces against it and make the infant laugh. Then the great sisters would send them flying, for it was time for the growing god to sleep.

They did not speak of his birth or how he'd come to the grotto; his nature was restless and discontented and such knowledge would not have improved it. So when Hephaestus

4

asked how he had come to be, lovely Thetis thought it best to tell him that in the very beginning of things there was nothingness . . . a dreamless sleep. Then it was Eurynome who first awoke, put out her foot and found no place to rest it. So she divided the sea from the sky and danced naked on the wave. (Here Eurynome, who like her sister was but in the first blush of eternity, laughed and half-shook her head.) But it was so, Thetis insisted, and as Eurynome danced, a wind sprang up behind her. It was the north wind that gets all creatures with child.

Hephaestus stared at Eurynome. His eyes were bright, and in them Eurynome saw an image of herself and her wild, lonely dance. Discontent left him and he seemed to forget what had troubled him most.

Then, through the crystal window, he began to see and take note of the wild and passionate embracings of the sea-nymphs. He watched the sinuous coilings of deep creatures as they coupled. He was excited and bewildered. His dreams were all awry. Discontent returned, and the grotto grew dark with his scowls.

So Eurynome herself decided that it was time for the ugly little god to know that he had come from high Olympus, and—

'Olympus? What is that?'

'It is a mountain in the sky, Hephaestus, where the gods have their home.'

'Who are the gods?'

'Children of the Titans who once ruled the universe.'

'Tell me how they came to be and what became of them. Tell me who was before them, Eurynome; for Thetis says you were first of all. Is it so, Eurynome?'

The goddess smiled. For a long while she said nothing. Little by little, the smile left her face, and shadows drifted across her brow. Then she began, and the walls of the grotto seemed to roll away as her words unmade them. She told of a thick, dark void, full of roaring and struggling. It was everywhere, and vast commotions banged and thundered as the unseen elements fought, one against another. Such was Chaos.

Then a single spirit, no one knows which, plucked the elements apart and separated them even as the sea-nymphs and the turtles separate the weaving ferns that tangle their paths through the dark sea. Up and up soared the aether, dividing away from the hanging air. All that was heavy sank below. For a while it seemed to dance—as the sand dances in the wake of the sea-horses before it slowly settles. Then earth became firm and solid and lay at last in the arms of ocean, heaviest of the elements.

Now came a marvel even more wonderful. Deep in Chaos, clogged in its thickness and night, there had been certain immortal seeds. They began to grow. Nourished by earth and air they grew into huge glittering beings who seized command over all the universe. They were the seven Titans.

'Are you listening, Hephaestus?'

The child looked up. He had been playing with his pearls and beads, and arranging them in patterns like the weeds and fishes he had observed through his window.

'Will you hear more?'

For a moment he searched for more pearls to finish his design; then, finding none, nodded.

'The tale is dark and fearful, Hephaestus. Will it give you bad dreams?'

'Will they be worse than the dream of falling, falling, falling?'

Eurynome frowned, and looked up so that her eyes seemed to pierce the grotto's roof and accuse the sky. Then she stretched out her hand and gently stroked Hephaestus's harsh black hair.

'You must ride the nightmare, child, even as it plunges. You must break it till it answers the rein and flies.'

The child shook his head free of the goddess's hand, and fixed her with his savage eyes.

'The fearful tale. Give me another nightmare to ride.'

The king of the seven Titans was Uranus, and in that ancient time he had seized the earth for his garden. He planted it and tended it till the mountains and valleys were all green and gold in an endless spring. Then Uranus lay with Mother Earth and she brought forth a second race of Titans, who were as harsh and savage as the rocks from which they had sprung. Among them were the one-eyed Cyclopes and the hundred-handed giants: craggy monsters who, in the stillness of night, resembled great configurations of land. Violent in their pride, they rebelled against their father. But they lacked his power.

Uranus flung them into a deep, fearful hole called Tartarus. For nine nights and days they dropped like struggling black mountains, till at last they were extinguished in echoing shrieks and groans.

Uranus listened and smiled. There was nothing in heaven and earth that could oppose him. His throne was the very rock of the universe. He closed his eyes and the sun and stars went out. He slept and dreamed that Mother Earth was in his arms. He saw her smile; he heard her sigh. His huge hands tightened till he dreamed her breath came sharp and passionate.

He could even hear each separate intake, which seemed to catch at its return with an almost secret air; and he heard the beating of her heart. But he slept on, and a single lamp cast his heaving shadow against the soaring wall of his bedchamber. The lamp flickered, making the sleeping shadow writhe to the rhythm of his dream.

The beating heart, the hissing breath—they were coming nearer. The flame leaped and danced at the wick. The shadow bulked and cowered, for another shadow had joined it. A dreadful, creeping shadow, at first like a bird with one wing upraised. But it was not a bird. It was Cronus, his eldest son, and the wing was a huge stone sickle!

Uranus opened his eyes and the universe blazed up all round him. Then Cronus struck. And it all went out for ever. Not even his dying scream was heard, for it was drowned in Cronus's mighty shout of triumph. The terrible king was dead.

Doors and passages in the great stone castle rang and thundered as the Titans proclaimed his still more terrible son. They tore dead Uranus in pieces and cast them into the sea. They grinned and laughed and joked as they watched the dark sea crack in a hundred places to let the multitude of Uranus in. Then it closed up after, as if he had never been.

But the ocean could not hide what had been done. Three drops of blood from the death wound had fallen unnoticed on the earth, and silently there rose up three terrible creatures. At first they stood still and quiet in the shadow of the castle's southern wall. They might have been dwarfish trees—or bushes, even, with smooth black foliage that hung down like cloaks. But there was movement among what might have been their topmost twigs, as if some breeze was ruffling them. They were nests of snakes, spitting and twisting as they grew out of shadowy heads. Then, of a sudden, they swayed. The black foliage spread into wide, jointed wings. Once, twice, they beat the air; then the three creatures rose up. Round and round the castle they flew, and their shadows seemed to scratch and scar the stones. They would know that place again. Then they vanished into the upper air. They were the Furies—avengers of fathers murdered by their sons.

Cronus slept in his father's bed, with Rhea, his sister-wife. His dreams were easy and seemed to hang in thick curtains across his mind. Suddenly he awoke, as if the curtains had shifted. He stared uneasily into the dark, but saw nothing. He closed his eyes and tried to smile away whatever had disturbed him. But it would not go. There was, or seemed to be, a rustling and a creaking in the air and a smell of snakes. He turned on his back and looked up. Nothing. Yet some drops of moisture fell on his face. They burned like venom, and he cried out in fear and disgust. He did not sleep again that night.

Next night the Furies came again. They looked down on the new king, smiling in his sleep. Then with their curious sharp instruments they made another hole in the curtain of his dreams and whispered through it that he, like his father, would be ruined by his son. With the coming of the dawn, they flew away, but left the marks of their shadows behind. They would be back.

Night after night they came to visit Cronus, till his sleep hung in tatters and through every rent came the hateful words, 'Cronus, you will be ruined by your son! There is no escape!'

A wind blew through the king's head and all the exposed caverns of his mind began to ache and crack. Nothing comforted him—neither his throne nor his queen. All was swept aside by the nightly terror of the Furies and the threat of the unborn son. Despairingly, he embraced Rhea; then, with a cry of dismay, thrust her from him as he remembered that out of this chief consolation would come his chief danger.

Yet he could not endure without her, and at last she bore him a child. Proudly she brought it to him in swaddling clothes. The Furies' words roared a gale through his head. His

9

hands shook and madness finally seized him. He took the infant almost tenderly from the queen and thrust it, living, into his gigantic mouth. Then he laughed till his stone palace rocked on the mountain top. He had cheated the Furies.

That night they came again. But Cronus was ready and went for them with his bare hands. He clawed the air and beat the walls, but it was not till dawn that they flew away. He saw them like black moths dwindling in the sky.

The mad king grinned in triumph. Sooner or later, he would destroy his tormentors even as he had eaten his child. Nothing would shake his throne. So he kept spears in his bedchamber, and knives and arrows. They flew from the casements and scarred the walls as Cronus killed the air.

Then Rhea bore another child. Was there a traitor in his bed? No matter. Cronus was armoured at all points. Again he ate the child.

He would reign for ever.

Some more children after that the wild Titan swallowed. Yet each time he took them from her almost lovingly, so that Rhea's anguish was multiplied by hope.

Then at last she bore such a son as she could not endure to lose. He shone like a star, and her heart ached as he smiled unknowingly.

'Fetch me the child!' she heard the mad king shout. 'The child! The child!'

With trembling hands, she hid the infant among the bed-clothes, then stared round desperately. Beside the door was a stone that wedged it open in the heat of the day. Its size was the size of the child. Hastily she wound it in the swaddling bands over and over . . . .

A shadow darkened the doorway. Rhea looked up. Cronus stood before her. 'Give me the child!' Cronus's eyes flickered over the tumbled bed linen. Frantically Rhea clasped the swaddled stone. He held out his arms. 'My son! My son!' he half whispered, half groaned, and opened wide his mouth. Rhea turned away. Terror seized her. The bedclothes were stirring. Fearfully she looked back at her husband. Had he seen it? His eyes were hooded and remote and his hands hung empty at his sides.

He reached out and stroked her cheek. Then he wiped his

mouth and left the room.

When he was gone, Rhea sank to her knees beside the bed. She stared into the careless folds. Then she started. Two golden eyes were gazing out at her, and an infant's lips were curved in a prophetic smile.

2● The War of the Gods and Titans

'Was he a god, Eurynome?'

Hephaestus, in the grotto under the sea, stared into the goddess's eyes. But she seemed lost in thoughts and memories, and did not answer.

'Yes, he was a god.' It was gentle Thetis who spoke. She stretched out her hands, and Hephaestus shambled towards her and crouched at her knee. She smiled with pleasure and told the ugly little god of how this shining child was taken secretly to a cave on the island of Crete. Here there lived children of the Titans and the earth. They were strange, quick, wild creatures, like sinews of the air. They were the nymphs and spirits of the woods and streams. Into the care of these nymphs the child was given. They brought him mountain honey to eat, and hid his cries under their songs, so that Cronus should not hear him.

'What was their song, Thetis?'

Thetis sighed, and in a lilting voice she sang the song the nymphs had sung to the infant . . . and the wild music of the sea rushing through the conch shell accompanied her. Beyond the window the sea-nymphs listened, and the Sirens learned her song.

Hephaestus's eyes were closing.

'What was his name?' he mumbled dreamily.

'Zeus.'

But the god's eyes were shut, and the name hung emptily in the air.

How long he slept, there was no way of measuring; neither night nor day visited the grotto under the sea. Then he awoke, and the name of Zeus was on his lips. So Thetis told him more tales of Crete and Mount Ida where the infant grew to manhood. She told him of how, when tiny, the clever nymphs hung his cradle from a branch so that Cronus should find him neither on the earth nor in the sky. Then she told of how, in the dark nights, the flash and glimmer of his growing limbs might be seen as he moved among the foliage of Ida's trees. And always she ended her tales with the song the nymphs had sung . . . and Hephaestus drifted away into dreams. But always among them there galloped the nightmare that flung him from its back so that he awoke with the desolate cry of one who had fallen from a high place.

His ugliness increased. He was misshapen, having vast strength in his shoulders and arms and great weakness in his legs. His discontent became fierce and violent. There seemed no outlet for it till Thetis gave him an anvil and hammer to play with, and Eurynome made him a forge. Then he was able to vent the fury of his nature on metals that knew no pain.

The goddesses brought him gold and silver and watched as he hammered and twisted them into shapes as tormented as his own. His brows furrowed and his eyes retreated into the recesses of his head. At last the metals began to obey him and the monster chuckled with delight.

Wonderingly the goddesses saw there was a second nature in Hephaestus far deeper than the first. As there was no mirror in the grotto, his vision was untarnished by sight of himself. It was uninterrupted beauty that came from the forge as he rendered into changeless metals the changing marvels he saw.

Bracelets, necklaces, combs and buckles he made for the two goddesses, jointed and lapped together as marvellously as the gleaming scales of the sea-creatures that jostled the crystal window. He made sandals, silver for Thetis and gold spun as fine as the bending ferns for grave Eurynome, with designs of waves upon them as if to remind her of the time when she'd danced on the first wide sea.

But the loveliest thing he made was a brooch. In silver, drawn and beaten till it seemed like foam, he had imprisoned a sea-nymph and her lover, coiled and twined in a pearl and coral embrace. All the wild and urgent passion of creation was in this little brooch . . . and a strange new tenderness besides.

'Hephaestus!' whispered Thetis. 'If Olympus only knew what a god they have lost to the sea!'

She stretched out her hand for the marvellous brooch. But ugly Hephaestus drew back. He scowled with all his old savageness and ill-temper, and limped to the furthest part of the grotto where he leaned, panting, against the rock. He stared at the goddesses who had nursed him, and had brought him this far in the tale of Creation.

'What more is there?' he muttered. 'Why am I lost to Olympus? Who am I?' His ragged brow shone with sweat, as if he was trying to drag the answer out of the air. 'Why do I always dream of falling?'

He raised the brooch threateningly. 'Tell me or I will destroy it!'

There was silence in the grotto. No sound was heard save for the soft roar of the waters through the conch, and, far, far away, the silvery voices of the Sirens as they sang the song they'd learned from Thetis—the very song that had once lulled the infant Zeus upon Mount Ida, long ago.

Then grave Eurynome raised her eyes and stared across the grotto at the brutish infant, who scowled like the rocks against which he crouched. Then her eyes shifted, and she seemed to be looking beyond him, back to an ancient time. It was as if the tormented child's question had been no more than a reminder of something that had happened long ago. She began to speak, and though her voice was gentle, the air seemed to turn chill and bleak and the fire of the little forge flickered into dust. Once more the walls dissolved as Eurynome told the monstrous story of Zeus and his mad father, Cronus.

When Cronus slept, dreams of old Uranus would visit him so that he would awake, groaning and struggling, with a violent pain in his left hand—the hand with which he'd seized his father when he'd murdered him with the sickle. He would lie sweating in the darkness and the air would be filled with the sound of beating wings and the stench of snakes. He would stare and stare till his eyes all but burst from his head. Then a wing would scrape across them, and he would turn with a scream and entomb his head in his pillow, on which in the morning would be drops of blood. As always, the Furies parted with the dawn. But now, as they blackened the casement with their going, they left behind their whisperings, to creep and rustle in every quiet corner. 'Vengeance is near. Soon it will strike . . . soon . . . soon. . . .'

The mad king would stumble from his bed and glare out on the quiet dawning world. Fearfully, his eyes would range the shadowy valleys and mysterious mountains, whose shapes resembled formidable monsters. . . . What was that? A flash and glimmer among the foliage on Mount Ida. He had seen it before—several times—but never more than a glimpse, and then it had gone. Yet it seemed to menace him. What was it . . . so quick and horribly bright? Nothing, nothing. All was in his shattered mind. . . . Stop. There it was again: as always, on Mount Ida.

He shouted for his guards and bade them search the mountain and destroy whoever they should find. Hurry—hurry, before it is too late!

The guards went, and Cronus gnawed his lip until they returned. But they had found nothing on the mountain: only some bears and a strange serpent that flashed as it writhed away. Could it have been the snake that the king had seen?

Next night Ida was in darkness. No uncanny glimmer broke among its foliage nor moved among its trees. And most marvellous of all, the Furies did not come. For the first time since he had murdered his father, Cronus slept long and without dreams. He awoke with a start in fiery sunshine. The pain in his left hand was gone, and his only discomfort was a curious thirst.

He called for a cupbearer to fetch his honied drink. But his thirst was not quenched. Indeed, it seemed to have been increased by drinking. So a second cup was fetched. He drained it and laughed uneasily. What was thirst after the nights of the Furies? He flung the engraved cup across the room, where it cracked and splintered against the wall. A third cup! The king was still thirsty. 'Quickly! Quickly!' He cursed the cupbearer for a creeping fool. Then Rhea, smiling gently, rustled in to calm her lord. Behind her came another cupbearer, with another cup. 'Here, Cronus, my lord! Drink! The king must not go thirsty! Drink to your heart's content!'

So Cronus took the cup and drank.

He drank with barely a glance at the strange cupbearer, and the drink was rushing down his throat before an oddness struck him. Though he stood in Rhea's shadow, this cupbearer seemed to shine as if by the light of another, secret sun. And in that same instant he saw a look exchanged between Rhea and the stranger whose shining seemed suddenly menacing. The drink tasted sharp, and his throat began to sting and burn. But it was too late, he had drained the cup. Rhea smiled, and the cupbearer smiled; and Cronus knew that they had poisoned him.

'Who—who are you?' he whispered. The stranger's radiance seemed to increase till Cronus could not endure to look at him. 'Who—are—you?'

'Ask of the Furies, Cronus.'

Cronus opened his mouth to scream for help—but no words came. His throat was on fire and needles of pain stabbed at his belly. He fell back as cramps seized him and he began to retch. Wider and wider stretched his gigantic mouth till he felt the tendons split and tear at their roots. There was a tumult in his head—a mighty uproar. The bones of his gaping mouth were cracking and splintering as they were forced apart. And all the while, in his dreadful agony, he saw Rhea, his wife, and Zeus, his son, staring down on him with implacable hate.

Then Cronus began to vomit. Six times the poisoned Titan erupted and, like some shaking mountain, spewed out the fiery inhabitation of his belly. At last it was over; and Cronus stared in dread at what he'd brought forth. They rose up before him like columns of fire; the children he had consumed. In their midst, mockingly cradling the fatal stone with which he'd been deceived, was Rhea. 'Behold your sons and daughters!' she shouted. 'Behold the avenging gods!' Cronus shrieked and fled.

He fled high up among the granite mountains, stumbling and calling to the universe for help. At last he reached his fortress, and it was there that Atlas and all the Titans of the old order joined him in the war to destroy the gods.

Some say that this war raged for ten years; but there was no certain way of measuring it. Night and day were so obscured that time itself was blinded and could no more than mark the tempests, earthquakes and scalding storms of the battles. Huge mountains were plucked from the earth and hurled like pebbles against the sky, where they made black holes in the milky fabric of the stars. Again and again the gods approached the fortress of Cronus, and again and again they were beaten back.

In angry despair, Zeus stared up at the mighty stronghold that seemed to have become a part of the very sky. Then he remembered something that the timeless nymphs of Mount Ida had told him—for they were not always singing. They had told him of certain ancient prisoners who still lingered in Tartarus—the Cyclopes and the hundred-handed giants, tremendous children of Mother Earth, who had been forgotten by Cronus in his madness and pride. Even now they raged and rotted in their chains. Even now they waited.

With his brothers Hades and Poseidon, Zeus went down into Tartarus. Through the groves of black poplars and across the wide dark river Styx the three gods moved like flickering flames. Further and further into the dreadful region they voyaged, passing among steaming rocks and between tall cliffs of jet. Now the air grew foul and thick with fog. Briefly the three gods glinted in and among it. Groans and harsh weeping echoed all about them, together with the grinding of chains. Then the air rifted as if worn threadbare by agony and gloom, and through the holes and rifts the gods saw the gigantic prisoners, chained to the everlasting cliffs. There hung the unbelievable hundred-handed giants, enmeshed in iron; and beside them, so huge that they towered to the height of the cliffs, were chained the Cyclopes in each of whose single eyes was such pain and despair that even the gods were appalled.

Swiftly the brothers freed them and led them up out of Tartarus. They crossed the river Styx and passed through the groves of black poplars beside the ocean. So vast was the bulk of the creatures who had been freed that in the darkness the gods seemed like moving stars, followed by a second, blacker night. At last they came to the mountain of Cronus, and the three gods greeted their three sisters who had awaited them. Together the children of Cronus stared at their terrible allies.

The strange eyes of the Cyclopes, set in their heads like monstrous jewels, glinted faintly in the starlight. For the first time since the days of old Uranus they were smiling. They stared up at the fortress in the sky; then they nodded and gave the gods the weapons they would need. To Hades they gave the Helmet of Invisibility, to Poseidon they gave the Trident that shakes the earth, and to mighty Zeus they gave the Thunderbolt before which all must fall.

Hades put on the helmet. At once he faded so that where the grim god had once stood, was now no more than a shadow such as might have been fancied by a tired eye. Quietly this vague shadow began to drift up the mountain towards the lofty fortress, and the armed gods followed stealthily after.

A little apart, but following the same course, moved another shape . . . rapid and skipping, but curiously formidable. It leaped the crevices, then vanished in the shadows. Was it an ally—or was it a spy?

The mad Titan sat on his throne. Not even the Furies could torment him any more. He and tall Atlas had sworn to tear the universe to tatters before they would yield up a single star of it. Ten years was it since the war had begun? What was ten years to beings as vast as Titans? No more than a day in their great span.

Sometimes Cronus fancied that the ghost of his father, old Uranus, was in a darkened corner, squealing and gibbering for revenge. Indeed, he imagined much. He imagined that Rhea, his wife, was still by his side; he imagined that he was young again and that his father still lived and ruled and tended his garden, the earth . . . and the Furies were no more than tame birds who mistook his eyes for crumbs. Yet he knew all was in his mind.

A faint shadow seemed to drift through the opened window. Cronus shook his head. His eyes were tired. There had been no shadow. Quiet sounds seemed to scrape across the floor. Cronus sighed. He heard many quiet sounds inside his head. He leaned back against his throne. Beside him lay his mighty spear and the horn that would summon all the Titans and the elements themselves, should he have need of them.

He fancied the horn trembled and began to stir as if of its own accord. He closed his eyes. They saw many strange sights these nights and days, and he knew he'd but to close and open them for the dream to be dispelled. He opened his eyes. His horn and spear were gone. He looked up.

Hades stood before him! He shrieked—and turned away.

Huge Poseidon was there, with the trident aimed at his breast!

'Dreams—dreams!' screamed the ruined Titan, and twisted to shut them out. Then all the world blazed up as he saw the fiery Zeus. He crawled and tumbled from his throne even as the thunderbolt struck and split it to the mountain's root.

'Dreams—dreams!' moaned Cronus, lying in the ruins of his power.

But the roar of the thunderbolt had roused the Titans. With mighty Atlas at their head, they came storming in to save their king. Out-numbered, the gods drew back. Sudden victory seemed changed to sudden defeat. Then in through the huge casement skipped the shadowy form that had followed the gods up the mountain.

Half goat, half god, it grinned with savage joy. It opened its bearded mouth and gave a mighty shout. It was a shout such as no ear could endure nor brain withstand. It was a shout that had come from Chaos. It pierced the Titans' heads and called them back into the old, blind uproar from which they'd sprung.

Then, each driven wild by his own dark fears, the Titans fled before the grinning goat-god whose name was Pan, the maker of panic. After them rushed the hundred-handed giants, every hand an engine of fury and revenge for their grinding imprisonment. The reign of the Titans was over; the reign of the gods had begun.

Pan vanished as mysteriously as he'd appeared. None knew for certain who he was. Some say he was a foster-brother of Zeus; some say he was older, far older. . . . He went back to the fields and woods of Arcadia while the gods hunted down the enemy Titans, one by one. Rhea and her sisters were spared; also the mighty Prometheus and his brother, who had shrewdly taken no part in the war. Titans though they were, there was a grandeur about this gigantic pair that made even Zeus hesitate. They were left in peace to find themselves such homes as the ravaged earth could offer. But the rest were imprisoned in hateful Tartarus where the hundred-handed giants still watch over them with eternal eyes. Last to be seized was the great Atlas, whose punishment was harshest of all. He was con-demned to hold up the sky on his shoulders for as long as the gods should reign. At last the Furies' prophecies had been fulfilled and murdered Uranus had been avenged.

3 ● The Fruits of Power

The gods in their victory ranged the wide universe till they chose as their home Mount Olympus whose peak hung in the clouds. Here they fashioned their palaces and a great council chamber with ivory columns and a golden floor. It was in this council chamber that the three mighty brothers drew lots from a helmet for the three realms. Here, Hades drew the underworld, home of shades and the unborn dead; here great Poseidon drew the sea and all that lay beneath it; and here Zeus, lord of them all, drew the lot that gave him sovereignty over the boundless sky. But earth, the fair garden of old Uranus, was awarded to none of them; Zeus decreed it free to all.

Then Zeus turned to the three eternal sisters and gave them their powers. To Hestia, lovely, gentle Hestia, he gave dominion over all homes and the peace within them. To marvellous Demeter he gave the harvests and the fruits of the garden earth. Then he turned to the last goddess—who should have been the first. He turned to blazing Hera, mightiest of the three.

This was not well done. The radiant god, overcome by the largeness of his gestures, had overlooked his chief sister. What was there left for her?

Hestia and Demeter, already satisfied, looked to Zeus with reproach. How could he have forgotten Hera? Poseidon and Hades looked away. Then Zeus, great in all things, smiled on the mighty lady. 'And to you,' he said grandly, 'nothing less than the king himself. To you I give the—the queendom of the sky. To you I give myself. You shall be my wife, Hera—'

He opened his golden arms, and the godlike smile was still upon his lips. There was a silence in the council chamber. Even the clouds that drifted past the inlaid casements seemed to pause uneasily. The god's smile remained unanswered; his arms unfilled.

'You shall be my wife, Hera.'

But Hera made no answer. Her face was dark with anger. She had been slighted. She swept from the high council chamber, her rich robes flying and her eyes afire. Awed, the gods watched her go—then turned to the king of the sky who stood, with golden arms still outstretched.

He frowned and a night of angry shadows filled his eyes. He was lord of the sky, and he was lord of the gods. He would be Hera's lord if he had to scour the universe to find and subdue her.

She was gone from Olympus. Torn threads of cloud wisped down the steeps to mark the haste of the goddess's passing. Trees leaned and the tops of high groves were scorched by her anger. Zeus followed after like a fiery meteor, dispelling all shades and darkness so that Hera might have nowhere to hide.

He asked of the earth-spirits and the sisters of Rhea if they had seen her—but none could or would tell him where Hera had fled. So he quenched the fury of his passion upon them and then passed on. Themis he left to bear him the Seasons, and on Mnemosyne, nymph of Memory—who was subtle enough to hold him for nine nights—he begot the Muses.

At last he came to the mountain where Cronus, his father, had fought his last battle. The ruined fortress still stood. Zeus looked up and saw a radiance gleaming from the ancient casements. He had found her.

Once before the fortress had fallen to him; now it would fall again. He began to mount. Then, half way up, he paused. His brow furrowed as he brooded and stared up at the bulk of the walls against the darkening sky. How to breech them—how to bring them tumbling down . . . ? He smiled. . . .

Alone in old Cronus's throne-room, Hera looked out on the night. Her fury was undiminished; she burned with anger against Zeus. Never would she accept him. She would remain a virgin for all eternity, and shine barrenly in a lonely sky.

She sighed and leaned against the cracked and crumbling casement. Suddenly she heard a faint, melancholy sound. She started—and smiled. It was a cuckoo, somehow lost high on the granite mountain. Softly she called to it, and the little bird came fluttering to her hand. It was thin and wretched-looking, with feathers awry. It seemed to have flown a great way in search of a nest.

'Come, little bird,' murmured the goddess. 'You and I will share our loneliness in this high place. Come—here is a nest.'

She took the bird tenderly, and warmed it in her bosom—

She cried out! She struggled . . . even fought! But it was too late. She had been deceived. The air was full of golden laughter as Zeus resumed his godlike shape. 'You shall be my wife, Hera!' he whispered triumphantly, and held her in arms from which there was no escaping. So Hera gave up the unequal contest, and gazed at the great god with deep, prophetic eyes.

Now the night took on a velvet darkness such as no night has known before or since. It was a curious, soft darkness that seemed to ease the world. There was nothing frightening about this darkness, yet it was full of mystery and strange, subtle noises. There was gentle laughter everywhere—and sudden, tender moans that dissolved into sighs and murmurings. . . .

Nor did this strange night give way to day as other nights had done. It lingered and drifted on and on as Zeus and Hera, on the mountain top, embraced in this, their vast bridal night. At last it was the sun who wearied of waiting and crept up over the mountain to shine on the green and golden world. Then Zeus and Hera rose and returned to Mount Olympus, king and queen of the sky.

Immortal Zeus had conquered; but Hera walked the court-yards of heaven with a still prouder air than his. She was with child.

Often Hera talked with her sisters of the glorious infant that was growing within her; of how it stirred as if with longing for its immortal destiny. Sometimes she smiled as she remembered the passion of Zeus and of how he had drawn out the night so he might enjoy her infinite charms. Not Zeus but Hera had conquered; and the witness of her conquest was the child she carried, the child it had taken so enormous a night to make.

Then at last her labour began, and it was as tremendous as the child's begetting. Hera's cries rent the sky and all creation waited. At last there came one mighty shout of joy; the child was born!

The shout was heard in the woods and fields where Goat-Pan and his nymphs paused and smiled. It was heard in the dark underworld where grim Hades sighed. It was heard beneath the sea where Poseidon harnessed his brazen-hoofed horses and yoked them to his chariot of gold. Then all the gods mounted up to Olympus to honour Hera, mother of the new-born god.

She lay back with closed eyes and the infant hidden at her breast. She heard the immortals coming; the chamber was filled with strange perfumes and the murmur of expectation.

She opened her eyes. 'Behold!' she cried. 'Behold the child of Hera and Zeus!' She lifted the babe from her breast and held it up for the gods to wonder at.

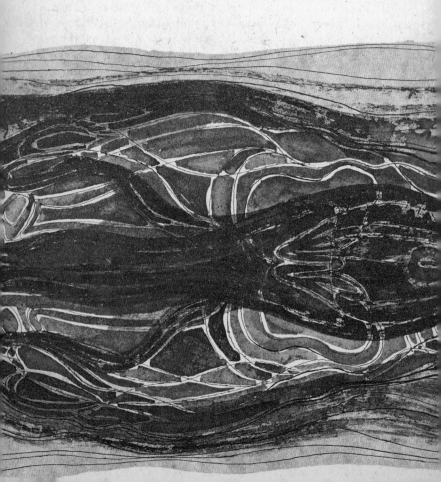

Silence. Their wreathed faces seemed touched with stone. They were staring; their golden eyes were crooked. What was wrong? Uneasily, royal Hera turned the child about and looked on it for the first time. She caught her breath. The pain, like a vulture's beak, tore at her breast as her proud heart cracked.

The child was hideous. The mighty passion of the king and queen of Heaven had brought forth a misshapen monster.

She groaned and the sound was terrible. Then she rose from her childbed and went towards the arched casement, her eyes blazing with savage tears. She lifted up the tiny creature and, after a single kiss, hurled it out into the sky. It glittered in the wide clear blue, seeming to hesitate a moment as if it would fly back; then it began to fall and fall, its shrieks and screams diminishing as it dropped down, down, down towards the sea.

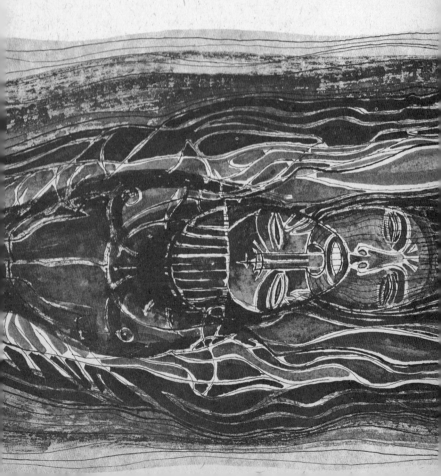

4● The Springtime of the Gods

There was a silence under the sea. Thetis and Eurynome stared at the god they had saved, who crouched against the cold, rough wall like some tormented memory, frozen in its ugliness.

Suddenly there was a sound of something dropped. Thetis gave a cry of dismay. The brooch—the marvellous brooch had fallen from Hephaestus's hand. Now it lay on the grotto's floor. A piece had broken away. The little coral sea-nymph had been snapped off. Only her lover remained. Legs bent as he'd once straddled her and arms emptily outstretched, he resembled Hephaestus himself, limping, yearning after a broken dream.

Even as the goddess watched, a finger of the sea foamed across the floor and covered the nymph. Then it drew back and the wondrous thing was gone.

'Would you have saved me, Thetis,' muttered Hephaestus, 'had you known that my own mother had flung me from the sky?'

'I—I—' whispered Thetis, and then her words were lost in a wild bellow of rage and hate and pain, as the outcast child cursed his mighty mother. He beat the walls till the rock flaked and crumbled and his blistered hands hung in tatters. Then, little by little, his roaring grew quieter till it was no more than harsh groaning sighs.

'What will you do, Hephaestus,' muttered Eurynome, 'now that you know all?'

The god raised his head and stared up, up to the grotto's roof. His face, all seamed and scalded with tears, resembled that part of a furnace where the flames have reached their utmost fury and take on the aspect of eyes, nostrils and shuddering mouth.

'I will return. I will tear their mountain from the sky. I will—'

'Look! Look!' Thetis was staring through the crystal window. There was a disturbance in the sea. The ferns were bending as before an underwater wind; and the sea-forests trembled as multitudes of gleaming sea-nymphs and curious monsters rose up and fled. All the green world was in a commotion, and amid the bubbled currents swirled brief sparklings of white and gold.

Suddenly, the window was obscured. A massive shape of white and crinkled bronze was pressed against the crystal. It was too huge for its form to be seen entire. But it was curved and a fine downy hair seemed to dust it and dance in the swirling sea. Then it was gone.

'What was it, Thetis?'

'It was the little finger of Poseidon, child. And he is only the brother of Zeus. Do you still hope for revenge?'

Above the grotto the great sea rolled and rolled, so that, under the sun, its silken coverlet seemed to heave with unquiet dreams. But they were secret, and not even the waves that ceaselessly uncurled on the quiet sands betrayed what lay within.

The child that had fallen from the sky was forgotten as if he had never been. The gods looked down from Olympus and the sea looked up and gave them back only their own image. Proud and gleaming, the immortal mountain soared among the clouds.

It was the Cyclopes who built Olympus, in gratitude to the gods who'd freed them. Sweating under the sun, they raised the walls, set the roofs and paved the courts and avenues with gold and bronze. No mortar had been used but weight had answered weight so that trued and polished stones seemed mortared with air and had an aspect of soaring lightness, despite their eternal strength. And lest the imprisoned Titans should rise again, the Cyclopes stocked an armoury for Zeus of racked thunderbolts and two great silver bows, each with its quiver of sudden arrows winged with black.

From this colonnaded watchtower of the universe, the gods observed the quickening earth below. Goat-Pan hard at play with the nymphs had peopled the woods and glades of Arcadia with creatures not unlike himself. And these little guzzling Pans had leaped aboard each other and got stranger creatures still: rams and goats, deer and lions, queer spotted cats and snuffling boars that blundered tuskily in search of beds, enemies and truffles. . . .

The gods laughed—and pricked them on: then Zeus saw lovely Leto, a Titan's daughter, walking by a lake. At once there was a wind in heaven and a fiery light; and out of its eye flew a quail. Down sped the transfigured god, down to pensive Leto. With amorous screeches he flew at her again and again and, in a white passion of wings, quenched his restless heat.

But Hera had seen him; and when he returned in his smiling, god-like shape, he was not well met. Savagely, she turned on him for spending his seed on all but her. Then the queen of Heaven, in her black and scarlet robes, leaned out over the world; and presently down the mountain's steeps there writhed a huge, malevolent serpent. Through field and forest the monster glided, in pursuit of Leto, Hera's rival—for the Titan's daughter was already quick with child.

Leto's flight had begun, and the sound of her running feet and panting breath echoed across night and day. Wherever she rested, wherever she paused to drink or to crouch in some obscure shade, she heard the harsh scaly rustle and the venomous hiss of her pursuer. Her pace grew slower as the burden she carried grew greater and dragged her down.

At last she came to Delos and, in her extremity of fear and pain, stumbled into a cave. Her time was at hand.

With merciless eyes, Hera still watched from her Olympian chamber as her serpent coiled and nuzzled towards the cave. Beside her watched all-powerful Zeus.

'Why do you quail, great Zeus?'

The god withdrew his eyes as the monster, ever obedient to Hera's will, writhed and twisted at the entrance of Leto's cave.

'Why talk of quails, Hera? Do you not remember a cuckoo?'

Great Hera turned; and the serpent faltered and looped aimlessly in the grass.

Zeus laid a golden arm about Hera's white shoulders; drew her back towards the couch. The serpent hissed; its purpose was blinded.

The queen of Heaven smiled as Zeus's passionate face usurped the sky. . . .

The serpent moaned; its coils grew langorous; it slid away from the entrance to Leto's cave.

Presently there was a cry; it came from the darkness of the cave. It was a cry of sudden pain. Then came another, lower, sweeter, a cry of joy. Momentarily on high Olympus Zeus raised his head.

'What troubles you?' murmured Hera.

The father of the gods made no answer. Instead, he shook his head; and laughed triumphantly.

Far, far below, the surface of the sea broke up into a million ripples as if it would let the great god's laughter in. Then the ripples died and the waters resumed their desolate heaving as if some forgotten god in their depths was beating his fists against blind walls, knowing himself to have been doubly betrayed.

The sea-nymphs shuddered and clapped their hands to their ears; and the towered crabs clambered crazily away. As they went, they pincered up the delicate rubble of the ocean's floor: forsaken shells, green pebbles, and a curious piece of coral that resembled a nymph. On and on it went, now dropped, now caught up again; but always moving towards a certain shore. . . .

There was once a nursery on Mount Olympus, where the Muses taught the children of the wayward nymphs. Some were quick, some were sluggish, some were as careless as their mothers. But there were two who were none of these: a strange brother and sister of surpassing beauty, who learned as if they remembered, and whose eyes in their moments of dreaming turned always to the moon and sun.

From time to time the nymphs would come to claim their children and carry them off with amazement and delight. But none came to claim this brother and sister. Only a sadly beautiful Titan's daughter would sometimes wander through the glades and watch them at their glittering play.

At last Leto could endure it no longer. She stepped from her concealment and caught the children in her arms. She covered

29

them with tears and kisses and bade them seek their father and claim a birthright from him.

'Who is our father?'

Leto shook her head. Her eyes were filled with pain and fear.

'How will we know him? Where will we find him?'

'On the high mountain. Go, go.'

So the brother and sister set forth and travelled till they reached the foot of the mountain whose glimmering peak dissolved in the clouds. Hand in hand they climbed through the forests, crossed the streams and mounted the frowning face of the rock. As they moved, the sun touched them with fire, so that they seemed at times to be like two dancing flames, one silver, one gold. At last, they entered the region of clouds, where all was vague and undetermined.

These clouds were like curtains in which there were strange patterns, broken by shifting folds. Now they hid rock, now they swayed and opened out on measureless drops to the distant world below. But still the great pair climbed, upward and upward.

'Brother, look!' The last of the curtains had parted. A mighty palace hung before them. The doors were open, and a golden light blazed out.

'Sister, here is our father!'

Zeus, king of the gods, stretched out both his mighty hands.

'My children, welcome to your home. Ask what you will for your birthright.'

'Father, we would have the moon and sun.'

Briefly Zeus paused; then he nodded, and all creation shook in assent.

Artemis and golden Apollo had come into their inheritance, and from the armoury of Olympus they took the tall silver bows and quivers of black-winged arrows; for they were young and delighted in sport.

Hera smiled. Her rage against Leto was over and done with. Once more the queen of Heaven was with child, and she was resolved to be calm. She had not forgotten the monstrous fruit of her huge bridal night. This time nothing must be allowed to curdle the child within.

So it grew and grew at its own vast pace. Time and Nature

were then still young and loose in their dominion, and events were still fetched and carried according to their brightness and the will of the immortal gods.

Hera's great calm spread over the universe like a canopy; and mighty Zeus took further advantage of it to welcome home another child.

Grave and lovely was this newcomer, yet with a touch of fierceness, too. Her limbs were straight, her brow was lofty and everywhere she went she kept an owl on her shoulder whose immense inquiring eyes set Hera's nerves on edge. But the queen of Heaven kept calm. . . .

At first, Zeus said the giant Pallas was the newcomer's father; then, when gently pressed, admitted she was a child of Poseidon and a nymph. Poseidon denied it, so shining Zeus confessed to the still calm Hera that the new goddess had been born in a manner so remarkable that he'd hesitated to disturb her sacred pregnancy with so striking a tale.

He had been assailed by a violent headache as he'd walked by Lake Triton. Such a headache! He'd roared and raged—hadn't Hera heard him?

No.

Then—then it was Prometheus, that good Titan, who'd come to his aid. At once clever Prometheus had seen what was amiss, and it was he who'd made a deep incision in Zeus's temple—See! Is the scar still there?—and at once the goddess had sprung forth fully armed.

Hera stared at radiant Zeus. Then she looked at the grave fierce goddess and her owl. Wisely the newcomer held her tongue; so Hera shrugged her white shoulders and Athene, goddess of wisdom, was admitted to Olympus without more ado.

Almighty Zeus beamed; and stole another look at the ever-tempting world below. Sweet limbs shone and amorous eyes glittered from every glade and wood. So down he burned, again and again—sometimes as a bird, sometimes as a mist or shower of rain—or sometimes (though rarely), when the nymph of his instant need was not partial to showers or feathers, as his glorious self. And still Hera, cautious of the god within, kept calm.

So far and wide the great god ranged, plummeting now

like a meteor, now like a dove. Scattered cries of laughter and amazement would rise up from the engrossing shadows where he'd plunged and where he was for a while out of sight of Olympus. But one pair of eyes always watched him. Heavy, bitter eyes. They were the eyes of the mountainous Titan, Atlas, who groaned under the burden of the sky. This mighty creature looked on the world he'd lost with envy and with pain. His punishment was endless and made darker by the brightness that everywhere afflicted his eyes. He lived—if such a dreadful fate was part of living—for one thing alone. The only spark of pleasure in his dark heart was the sight of his child who still went free.

For Atlas had a daughter. Her name was Maia, and she lived in a cave in a sharp, blue mountain.

She was a maid of the mountains and stars. She sang as the water sings when it falls down the face of the rock, gathering in pools, lapping over and pursuing its lilting course till it dwindles into the green silence below. Her song was not unlike the song the nymphs once sang on Mount Ida, when Zeus was a tiny child. Or so Zeus fancied as he saw the naked Maia play. Pierced with sudden joy, the coursing god was halted. Briefly he faltered, hovered, then down he plunged, sideways to the wind.

Further to the south, great Atlas groaned. The aching weight on his shoulders gave way before the sharper weight on his heart. Helplessly he watched his daughter engulfed in his enemy's fiery embrace. Try as he might, he could not close his eyes, but watched and watched till the lord of the sky was gone.

'O Maia, my daughter, my child!'

5 • The First Thief

There was a baby on the sharp blue mountain.

He was wrapped in soft skins and cradled in a leaf. He chuckled and gurgled and sometimes waved to the sun and the sky. Then Maia, his mother, would laugh and shake a finger, which he would seize as if he would steal it. So Maia would undo his fingers and sing to him the only song she knew. When at last he was sleeping, she left him to his dreams, with the mountain for his nurse.

For a moment she paused and looked back. She fancied the child had smiled—a curious, sidelong smile. Then she shook her head. It was not possible in one so young. She went on her way. Again she stopped. She thought she heard a sound of laughter, and quick plump feet. She shook her head once more. Some wild young mountain creature, not her darling new-born god.

'Cyllene! Cyllene!' she called to a nymph who served her. 'Go quickly to watch over my child.'

Cyllene turned to obey, and Maia murmured: 'But softly, for I think he is asleep.'

Now, belonging to the estate of the sun was a herd of cattle whose browsing gold enriched the pastures they fed upon. They bore the brand of mighty Apollo, god of the black-winged arrows and master of the sun.

Each morning as the sun-god rose he saw his cattle and westward scored their tally in shadows on the ground. So confident was the great god of this daily arithmetic that one day he was midway in the sky before he saw the fields were clean. His cattle were gone.

He stared and the earth sweated under his gaze.

33

He called them, but they did not appear. He shouted, in vain. A thief! A thief!

Blazing with fury, the great god left his chariot and came down into the field where his beloved herd had once grazed. He stared at the ground. Not even the marks of their hoofs remained.

His rage increased as he began his search. He peered into valleys, stared over mountains and along the banks of glittering rivers: but neither hide nor hair of his cattle was to be seen.

At last he came to Arcadia. He passed by a wood, full of the sounds of hiccoughs, chuckles and cracking nuts. Apollo's brows grew dark with contempt. He spread the branches and peered down into a clearing. There sat the fat, shaggy half-god Silenus, child of Pan. He was belching and telling wild tales to some dozen other satyrs like himself, but younger and not quite so fat. They drummed on the earth with their hoofs as they listened, chuckled and ate. Their chins were stained with berry-juice, and their strong yellow teeth were furred with half-chewed nuts.

One by one they turned their thick necks awkwardly as they felt the sun-god's gaze, till Silenus was left telling his tales to the unattending air. His coat was fuller and Apollo's radiance took longer to penetrate. Then at last he, too, turned, licked his lips and blinked uneasily into the sun-god's angry face.

'My cattle,' said Apollo, 'have gone.' The satyrs looked up at him with crafty innocence. 'Who has them?'

No answer; Silenus sadly shook his head.

Apollo's eyes pierced the depths of the woods. 'I will give you,' he said, 'a mountain of berries, grapes and nuts. I will give you warmth in the cold and light in the darkness. I will give you whatever your wild hearts desire if you will find my cattle—and the thief.'

Berries? Grapes? Nuts? Wild desires?

They grinned—and were off. They scattered through the wood—then beyond it, in all directions, and their hoofs sounded like diminishing hail.

All day they searched—then looked in alarm at the heavens. Night was in abeyance; the angry sun-god had not returned to his chariot; it still burned in a morning sky.

At last they came to a sharp blue mountain. They peered

up at its rocky sides. Silenus grunted. No place for cattle—not even the sun-god's. Then suddenly came a strange sound. It was a sound of music, but not like any they had heard before. It was a rippling, twinkling sound; very curious, very haunting.

'You go,' said heavy, fat Silenus, 'and come back and tell me what it is.'

So his companions scampered up the mountain, with grunts and cries and clattering hoofs. The music stopped as if frightened away. The satyrs stared at one another.

'What do you want?'

A nymph was sitting in the mouth of a cave.

'Nothing,' said a satyr. He belched and laid a hairy hand over his mouth. 'Heard music.'

'There it goes again,' said another, tilting his crooked head towards the cave.

They began to slip and shuffle, uneasy on their hoofs.

'What's delaying you?' came Silenus's voice, impatient, from below.

'A nymph.'

'Up there?'

'A mountain nymph.'

'I've seen them when I was young. They're as hard and cold as the rock. Come down!'

'The rocks are warm and soft when you're up here, Silenus. And so is she!'

Sounds of Silenus fidgeting below. A rough scrambling as if some fat creature was attempting to mount.

'Hush,' said the nymph. 'A baby is asleep.' She sighed. 'Such a baby! He charmed a tortoise from its shell. Alack, the tortoise died. But of that shell this marvellous baby made music. He strung it with cowgut—'

'With what?'

'Cowgut.' The nymph, her sweet tale interrupted, was sharp. *'Where did he get the cows?'*

And the sun still blazed in the sky.

The great charioteer, forgetful of the morning he had left unfinished, strode up to high Olympus. Over his shoulder were flung the skins of two of his cows. Nothing more had remained of them. Under his left arm, he carried something else.

With a pang of affection and alarm, Zeus saw it was Maia's new-born child.

Apollo, panting with haste and anger, threw down the skins of his slaughtered cattle at his father's feet; then, scarcely more gently, laid the infant on them.

'Here is the thief.'

The infant dug its tiny fingers into the rich red wool, and looked in innocent bewilderment from god to god.

'Who—me? I was born but yesterday.' He began to cry and, cupping his face with his hands, peered out from time to time to see if any hearts had been wrung.

Not Apollo's. The skins had been found in the infant's cave.

The infant turned to mighty Zeus. He spread out his little hands in a gesture of amazement and disbelief. Then Apollo pounced.

'See!' he cried, seizing one of the offered wrists. 'Red-handed!'

Zeus looked down. There was no doubt. The infant's guilty fingers were tipped with bright blood.

Zeus frowned. The infant, feeling himself to be overhung by two great clouds, smiled humbly at the lesser.

'Great Apollo,' he said. 'Only you could have found me out. No other god has half your skill.'

Apollo nodded, and almighty Zeus could not but feel proud of his new son's tact.

Then the child fumbled among the skins and drew out the tortoise shell, strung with the damning cowgut, that the sun-god had brought as further evidence. Apollo looked at it curiously.

'I made it specially for you,' said the child. 'Listen!'

He plucked the strings, and the music that the satyrs had heard sweetened the air of Olympus. It haunted the courtyards and the terraced walks, so that gods and goddesses, about their great business, paused to listen. Mighty Hera, aching from the child which was still growing within her, smiled and dreamed on the birth to come.

Then the infant began to sing. He sang of Apollo's beauty and Apollo's wisdom and Apollo's kindness—and Apollo's generosity to Maia's child. Then he finished, and the two clouds that hung above him had gone away.

36

The sun-god and his father smiled.

'Tell me,' said Apollo, 'how did you do it?'

'I bored holes in the shell—'

'No! My cows! There were no hoofmarks or anything.'

'Oh. . . . Yes. The cows.'

Then the child explained, with many a charming smile and sidelong glance at Zeus, how he had fastened pieces of bark to the hoofs of the sun-god's cattle, so that, wherever they went, no trace remained behind.

'But you may have my toy instead,' the child finished up, and held out the marvellous shell.

Apollo took it with a rueful smile.

'Keep the cows,' he said.

Idly, Apollo fingered the strings. He knitted his brows and began to discover a grave music. So intent was he that he did not observe the child. Consequently he was surprised when a new sound joined with his: a delicate crystal piping sound, that wove in and out of his majestic chords, like a fine silver tapestry. The child had another toy. It was a pipe, cut from reeds of subtly graded length. Apollo stared at it.

'I will give it to you,' said this remarkable child, 'if you will teach me how to tell the future.'

But here he had over-reached himself. Apollo took the pipe, but gave in return his golden staff with which he'd herded the cattle he no longer had. So the child, being small, new-born and defenceless, made the best of the bargain and took the staff.

'To learn the future,' said Apollo, feeling perhaps he had taken unfair advantage, 'you must go to the Muses on Mount Parnassus. They will teach you, even as they taught me.'

This done, Apollo declared himself satisfied and returned to his chariot still burning in the noonday sky.

'It has been a long morning,' said the new god to his father, and gave a sidelong smile.

Zeus sighed.

'I will not ask you what birthright you desire. I fear it would be too much. Instead, I will give you what I think is fitting. You shall be the god of thieves, sharp practice and fanciful make-believe.'

'And—' said the child.

Zeus laughed. 'And you shall be my messenger, if you

promise never to tell lies.'

'I promise, father, so long as I am not bound to tell all the truth. There must be room for fancy.'

Zeus laughed again and nodded his head in assent. Then he gave this new god a herald's staff with white ribbons. He gave him also winged sandals so that he might move with the speed of thought. He called him Hermes.

6● Desire

A brazen shout shook the heavens. Everywhere, in woods and fields, living creatures stopped, turned and stared.

A strange alarm filled every heart. A new light was burning on high Olympus. Hera's child was born.

Again the infant shouted—this time as his vast father held him up for all the universe to see. He was flawless; he was the unblemished son of Zeus. His father's radiance and his mother's pride marked his countenance and gave strength to his splendid limbs.

Vigorously he kicked in his father's arms—as if he would boot the stars out of the sky. . . .

Mighty Hera lay back on her couch and smiled. Her wretched first-born was quite blotted out in the glory of her second.

'Ares!' shouted Zeus. 'Behold Ares, my son!'

Now began the great procession, as all the gods and earth-spirits left their palaces and haunts to honour the new god on Olympus.

Goat-Pan combed the twigs and leaves from his shaggy hide, bent the forests aside and left his nests of shrieking, sighing nymphs.

Deep-thinking Titan Prometheus and his brother Epimetheus left their garden and, as they passed on their way, caught the tragic gaze of Atlas. Prometheus shivered as he sensed the force of the huge Titan's reproach; and he felt like a traitor to his race. Vainly he tried to pierce great Atlas's mind with what was in his own; but the one-time leader seemed turned to rock. So Prometheus hurried on to pay his homage to great Zeus's son; while his thoughts, as always, were elsewhere. . . .

Grim Hades harnessed his four black horses to leave the sullen underworld; and Poseidon the earth-shaker mounted

his golden chariot under the ocean and sent the sea-creatures scudding from his path. The sea-forests bent and swirled away before his coming, and the conch-shell at the entrance to the grotto of Thetis and Eurynome blared out the waters like a trumpet. Briefly, Poseidon leaned against the rock, resting his little finger idly against a curious crystal jewel, and bade a sea-nymph tell the goddesses of the grotto that Hera's child was born and that they, like all creation, must come to Olympus and honour it.

'What will be my son's birthright, great Zeus?' demanded Hera, leaving her couch and pacing her cloudy chamber. Through the tall casements she could see from afar the glimmering approach of the immortals, laden with blessings and, no doubt, gifts for Ares. . . .

'What will *your* gift be, almighty Zeus?'

The king of the gods smiled. The sun and moon he'd disposed of; likewise the harvests, the flocks, the sea and the underworld. Briefly he wondered if some distant star might stand in need of a lord?

Hera frowned. Zeus's smile did not deceive her.

'Your gift, lord of the sky? What shall it be?'

'Do not press me, Hera. When the time comes, my gift will not be found wanting.'

'What is there left, great Zeus, that you have not already given away? Must my son be idle while the creatures of your lust lord it everywhere?'

'Do not press me, Hera. Though you are queen of Heaven, remember that I am the king. Ares will have his birthright—when the time comes.'

With that, great Zeus left the chamber, brooding on what that birthright might reasonably be.

He paced the clouds and strode the universe; but no answer came. At last, he summoned Hermes, his messenger.

'Go,' he commanded the god of thieves and lies. 'Find me a gift for Ares.'

So immortal Hermes, quick as air and light as fire, flickered through the groves and forests in search of some bright, gaudy trifle. Something easily come by—yet looking as if worlds would not have bought it. Something that would do great credit to his own judgement, please mighty Hera and content her savage child.

Hermes did not like Ares. Though the new god was as handsome as could be wished, he was, in Hermes' eyes, a dull and surly brute. A loud voice and a powerful kick seemed to be the scope of his talents and the top of his wit. He was a fool; and Zeus's messenger abhorred all fools. . . .

Nonetheless—he flew on his winged sandals over Arcadia and the mountains to the west, dropping down whenever something glittered below. Here it was a hillside spring, there a forest pool that drew the thieving god. Once, he glimmered in a grove of myrtle . . . lingered, then flashed, laughing, on. What had he stolen? A nymph's maidenhead and her necklace of fine sea-pearls: both charmed away.

At last he came to the isle of Cyprus and rested on the wide, ribbed sand at the ocean's edge. The sun was rising and everywhere little land-locked pools of the sea flashed and shone and seemed to dance.

Hermes, forgetting all, was captivated. Pearls, diamonds, gold were all as nothing beside this humble water set in the inexpensive sand. If he could have done so, he would have lifted it entire, carried it to Olympus and fixed it on a chamber wall as a joy forever to behold.

He let fall the pearl necklace as thoughts strange and new flooded his supple mind. So absorbed was he, that he did not observe a great commotion that had sprung up in the midst of the sea.

The waters boiled and leaped and sprang aside. Large sea-creatures rose and flashed in the sun, turning over and away from the gushing deep. Then there erupted four gigantic white horses, streaming under veils of green, and the huge gold chariot of Poseidon reared aloft.

The sun stared down and seemed to water at the superior radiance of the god . . . and the outriding nymphs and Tritons, fiercely blowing the air, dissolved in a cloud about Poseidon's blaze.

Poseidon set his steeds towards Olympus and began to mount—great guest at the banquet for Hera's child.

As the chariot left the sea and the last linkages of water drained from its golden wheels, the commotion subsided and dispersed itself over the ocean. Great waves raced shorewards bearing in their teeth fragile shells and curious twisted pebbles —like messages from the deep. As they neared the shore, their speed diminished, their passion sank and they tumbled up on the sand, quite spent. Gently, they lapped by the pensive god of thieves, and plucked at his winged feet.

Hermes looked down. The waves had drifted the sand over the pearl necklace. But that did not concern him.

Instead, he gazed at what the sea had cast up. A piece of coral: a curious coral, with a faint, delicate blush.

Hermes picked it up. It was scarcely bigger than a thumbnail. In some marvellous and bewildering way, it resembled a nymph. See! There were her breasts, her belly, her enchanting, slender legs! There was her head, stretched back in a dreaming ecstasy, and her long hair coiling in a strange, intricate design. The god could even make out her face, like a tiny flower on the stem of her neck.

Who had fashioned this marvel—or was it but a chance of ceaseless currents under the sea that had so shaped the coral? And was it only in the god's imagining that the uncanny nymph had come to life?

Hermes brooded, but found no answer. The coral nymph troubled him and set up a turbulence in his infinite mind.

'Hermes! Hermes!' A distant thunder rolled down the sides of Mount Olympus. Zeus was summoning his messenger.

'Hermes! Hermes!' The thunder slackened to an angry rasp. Hermes half awoke from his dream. He stood up and gazed towards Olympus. Lightnings flickered and stabbed the cloudy heights. His great father was angry with waiting. So shrewd Hermes sped.

The sand rippled and danced vainly in his wake and covered the strange prints of his feet—for this young god left no tracks and moved with the speed and secrecy of thought. He met with Zeus on Olympus's slopes, where the rock gave way to trees, and where springs had their origins.

'Must I call twice, boy?'

'I came directly, great father.'

'Lies! I saw you dreaming by the sea. Not even Poseidon's noisy eruption disturbed you. What were your dreams, Hermes?'

'They were of—of Ares, sir.'

'Have you the gift? Have you done my bidding, little liar?'

Hermes held out his hand in which lay the coral nymph. The lord of the sky frowned. He took up the coral and stared at it.

'Who made this, Hermes?'

'The sea, perhaps. . . ?'

'Only the immortals can create.'

'But this is no creation. It is no more than a piece of coral. It neither grows nor lives—'

'It lives, it grows, Hermes—'

'In the mind, great Zeus. . . .'

'In the mind of a god.'

Zeus's eyes grew terrible with thought. He crouched above the tall trees and rested his head on his mighty hand. Wonderingly Hermes crouched beside him; and a strange expectancy fell upon the mountain and across the world beyond.

Springs gushed crookedly and smooth rivers overslid their courses as their guardian spirits turned from their tasks to watch the two gods brooding on the mountainside.

'Look yonder, child.'

Their eminence commanded an aspect of the sea. Great Hermes followed with his eyes the gaze of greater Zeus.

A curious motion had begun over the easy top of the waters. It concerned the foam with which the sea was always flecked. No matter how peaceful the waves, this foam never disappeared. It was silvery white and tended to lie in star-shaped clusters, never far from the shore. No movement of the waves had produced this foam; nor had it been forced up by currents passing through the vents and grottos of deep-sunk rocks. Its origins were more formidable. It was composed of the million bubbles of agony that had gathered round the fragments of murdered Uranus when they'd been cast into the sea so long ago. Nothing would disperse them. They clung to the surface of the waters like vague, broken memories. . . .

But now these flecks of foam were moving in a strange fashion. With immense speed they were coming together and forming a downy clot of whiteness. This was happening far out to sea—so far that it was not possible to distinguish foam from fine hanging mist. At times they seemed to be one, uniting sea and sky in a pillar of confused whiteness . . . now bending, now rising like a glinting waterspout such as Tritons, children of the sea god, sometimes blow to frighten the shrieking nymphs. . . .

Presently, flushes of pink and red began to stain the white, and a little stream of gold poured out as if from a spring, making intricate patterns in the disturbed air.

The veiling mists swirled and streamed, then bellied out as if some solid form within them had begun to move.

A faint sweetness drifted across the air and, as it reached the land, congregations of birds suddenly rose out of woods and groves. Tiny tattered clouds of wings—sparrows and doves—trembled above the trees. At first they circled—then they began to fly with intolerable haste toward the marvel in the sea.

They met it hard by the isle of Cyprus; and the hiding mists dispersed before the fury of their wings.

'Behold,' breathed Zeus, crouching still on the mountain-side with Hermes at his knee. 'Aphrodite, foam-born, goddess of desire.'

She rode upon a scallop shell and cast a smiling look at the brooding gods.

'Father,' whispered Hermes. 'Do you see how the sparrows and doves seek to be snared in her hair?'

Zeus made no answer but continued to watch as the smiling Lady of the Sea stepped ashore upon the isle of Cyprus. The last fold of mist fell away, and left her softly naked in the sun.

'Father—do you see where she treads? Flowers are growing —grass and flowers even in the barren sand!'

Zeus made no answer to the god at his knee. His head was bent, his eyes were deep and his fathomless mind reached regions even out of Hermes' scope.

'Father—see how she moves through the forests. See how the birds break themselves against the branches to follow her! See now! Wild beasts are leaving their lairs. Save her, father! Save your marvellous daughter! They will rend her—they will destroy her—'

But Zeus brooded on as leopards, lions and rancid wolves grumbled through bush and thicket after the glimmering Aphrodite.

Presently she stopped and turned.

The beasts whined and moaned. Their savage heads swayed this way and that, and their eyes grew huge and golden.

Then each with his own kind padded away into the shadows, accompanied by dreams.

Here, in secure darkness, they groaned and roared as they coupled, each with its dream.

Then Aphrodite laughed—and the sounds of the forest died away into a soft, purring sleep. Only the birds still sung, but piteously, for they were torn and injured from the sharp branches and, as they fluttered helplessly after the goddess, they dappled the leaves with their blood.

Now mighty Zeus rose and smiled down on his messenger. He held out his hand in which lay the tiny coral nymph.

'She lives, boy. Now she lives.'

7● The Birthday Party

The doors of Olympus were open wide; even so, there was scarcely room between the lintel posts for Poseidon's chariot to pass.

Ever early to come and early to go, the earth-shaker reined in his gigantic horses and turned them into the golden stables. Their hoofs clanged on the brazen floor . . . bronze on bronze, and the red sparks flew.

But Poseidon was not the first comer. Four stallions of dreadful black nodded plumed heads from their stalls; and at the sight of them, the sea-god's horses reared and seemed to claw the air. Grim Hades was the first guest at the banquet for Ares.

The brothers met in the great hall. This spacious place was the crown of the Cyclopes' labours, with its arched casements so widely pillared that the winged horses of the sun might have passed through without hindrance to hoof or blazing feather.

'You came in haste, brother,' said Poseidon, gazing across the star-paved sky and the world below it—as if the dark stain of Hades' journey still lingered. 'Why so eager to greet Hera's child?'

'Mine is a lonely kingdom, brother.'

Then the two gods stared enviously at the earth, the unclaimed kingdom where all the immortals were but visitors. Would it be given now to Hera's child, screaming Ares?

As the brothers dreamed and traced out the rich garden of Uranus where once the ruined Titans had held sway, the great hall began to gleam and murmur. The glimmering procession that Hera had seen from afar had reached Olympus. The huge, eager children of the universe were crowding in, bright-eyed

49

and full of the marvels of their travel.

Star-kings who'd galloped across the Milky Way; sea-nymphs and dripping river-gods who made no bones about avoiding the company of Poseidon, their surly over-lord; and the lively spirits who lived in the groves and glades of Arcadia. Goat-Pan was among them, his shaggy pelt sleeked down till it shone like a dappled waterfall on either side of his deep-cleft face.

Hermes greeted them and moved about the hall like a silver dream, smoothing rough edges, provoking ease; now smiling, now grave, now laughing with surprise.

Yes, yes, Ares would be among them soon. A strong god, golden as the sun. Handsome? Oh, indeed, yes. As handsome within as without, assured the god of tact and lies.

He drifted sideways to Prometheus and his brother. These two stood awkwardly apart, the last of the Titans among the assembly of gods.

'What will be the new god's birthright?' asked Prometheus, his haunted eyes striving to outshine the bland fire of Hermes' courtesy.

'Who knows what is in my father's mind?'

'The—the earth, perhaps?'

But the question glanced aside as Hermes flickered away.

'The birthright, boy. What is it to be?' Poseidon's harsh voice rasped in Hermes' ear.

'Only great Zeus knows, uncle.'

'The earth? Will it be the earth? Did your father remember his promise? The earth is for none of us. If he breaks his word, boy, there will be—'

Poseidon hesitated. A mighty movement in the hall distracted him. A crowding back—a sudden increase in light. They were coming, the Olympian family—blazing in power and beauty. Athene, vast Apollo and Artemis, Demeter and Hestia, majestic sisters—and in their midst, the lord of the sky and his queen with savage, frowning Ares, whose shout had shaken the stars.

'—war,' finished Poseidon, 'there will be war.'

The mother of Ares moved among her guests, praising and thanking each for the jewels and gilded toys they had brought. Hermes made a way for her, ever charmingly, murmuring a

50

path for her, stepping aside, stepping aside—the queen of Heaven . . . mighty Hera . . . my great father's wife . . . make way for the imperial lady of the sky . . .

'And what have you brought me, uncle?'

Ares plucked at brooding Hades, and pulled the dark god out of his dream. Greedily, Hera's child had been elbowing his way among the immortals to see what they might have brought him.

Hades smiled down at his infant nephew. 'Sweet Ares—my gift is in my deep kingdom. A dog. A fine strong dog with three heads. His name is Cerberus. He barks and waits on the farther banks of the River Styx. He runs back and forth; his eyes are like raw rubies and his three mouths gape for food. You shall come and feed him, Ares. Then you may stroke him and throw stars for him to fetch. He is a good dog, Ares . . . and he will love you well.'

'What shall I feed him with, uncle?'

A shadow, dark as night, came over the lord Hades' face. 'I will tell you when I know your birthright, Ares. What gift has your father laid up for you? What crown are you to wear?'

'Who knows what is in the mind of father Zeus?' murmured sudden Hermes, interposing between god and god.

Then the smooth messenger, with many a bending smile, began to draw Ares away from the company of his grim inquiring uncle.

'See, little Ares! See what Hermes has!'

The child struggled and frowned and made as if to roar; then the sun came out all over his golden face. He chuckled and snatched at the little coral nymph that Hermes showed him. Hermes laughed and held the nymph just out of reach. Ares stumbled after it. Hermes was charmed. Ares, despite his beauty, moved like a blundering boar. Laughter followed him everywhere and the child's face grew red with effort and dawning rage. Then, suddenly, he stopped.

'Give me that!' he shouted. 'A present for Ares!'

He clutched at a silver gown: reached up to a radiant breast over which danced a goddess's hair. The lady Thetis looked down as Ares sought to take her brooch.

This brooch was of silver, whipped and beaten till it resembled foam; and imprisoned in it was the tiny coral figure of some sea-lover, bent-legged as if crippled, half plunging forward as though bereft of a dream that had dissolved out of his embrace. There was an aching ecstasy in this little coral—a yearning of passionate despair.

Even Hermes was caught by the sweet pain of Thetis's marvellous brooch. Beside it, everything in the great hall and even in the universe beyond seemed vague and shapeless. . . .

'Gentle Thetis—it is lovely.'

Mighty Hera spoke. Drawn to the curious silence round her brass-voiced child, she too saw the brooch. She fidgeted with her own rich jewels. Though Zeus had ransacked creation to adorn her, she owned nothing that could compare with the sea-goddess's brooch.

Hera was seized with a piercing envy. She longed to ask Thetis what divine hand had shaped the brooch; what divine anguish had been so fondly expressed.

Then Hermes, as in a dream, lifted his hand and gently laid the little coral nymph under the lover's embrace. Once more he straddled her. His lameness took on a meaning and his arms were filled. Never was such an image of yearning so satisfied.

But not for fierce Ares. The child, seeing the coral nymph bestowed elsewhere, set up a roar and a screech of rage. The nymph! The nymph! He wanted the nymph—

He stopped. His voice echoed high in the lofty hall, shivering some wisps of cloud. Then the echoes died. There was silence. The immortal throng, previously so busy and murmurous, looked up and about. A strange sweetness was in the air; and a sound of beating and fluttering. Doves and sparrows were flying and chattering everywhere above them. Frantically they were topping each other, quite mad with tiny passion. They darted in and out of the vast casements, and, in passing, pecked at Athene's owl as if to prick the bird of wisdom into their own wild courses. The owl shut its eyes in pain and bewilderment. It hated the doves and the lecherous sparrows; it hated the new radiance that had come into the high, bright hall.

'The nymph! The nymph! I want the nymph!'

She came in robes of green and saffron, her soft form shining lightly through. She smiled with parted lips; yet contrived to blush as her gown shifted and opened to her step. Aphrodite, goddess of desire. . . .

'The nymph! I want the nymph!' roared the infant Ares—turning from the tiny coral image which had so marvellously come to life.

'For Ares! A gift for Ares!'

The sturdy child was quite beside himself with greed for the bright new goddess. He struggled to reach her. . . .

'Look—look! And him so young!'

'For shame!' Athene, Hestia and cold Artemis turned in blushing anger from the sudden plainness of little Ares' lust. He was indeed his mighty father's son. . . .

But Hera, in her imperial dignity, showed no concern. She loosed the child and let him run and tumble to laughing Aphrodite as if to a plaything.

The brooch. It still absorbed her, fascinated her. . . .

'Thetis. Who made it?'

The sea-goddess bit on her lip. Vainly she looked for her sister, grave Eurynome. But that mysterious goddess was with Zeus, deep in talk. Not to be interrupted.

'Lady Thetis. Who fashioned the brooch? Why are you silent when Hera asks? What do you fear? What do you hide in your grotto? Is it, perhaps, a child you have borne to some sea-creature's lust? A child of shameful birth but uncanny skill? Answer me, Thetis. The queen of Heaven commands.'

'Hephaestus made it.'

'Who?'

'Hephaestus.'

'I know no Hephaestus. Where is this—this shining one?'

'Under the sea, great Hera. In my grotto.'

Hera turned to Hermes, the messenger.

'Go, boy . . . go faster than the wind and fetch up this Hephaestus from the sea. Bring him to Olympus. Tell him the queen of Heaven would have him fashion brooches for her.' She cast an angry look on Thetis, who stood unhappily shifting her silver-sandalled feet. Hera observed them. 'And sandals, too. Be sure now, Hermes, to say that it is mighty Hera herself who bids him come.'

53

Helplessly, Thetis stretched out her hand; but it was in vain. Hermes, already on the casement, had leaped out into the boundless air, his winged sandals flashing like dropping stars. Rapidly he dwindled till he was no more than a silver speck. Then far, far below the goddesses saw the tiny green and white flurry as he pierced the surface of the sea.

'What god are you?'

Ugly Hephaestus, alone in the grotto, stared at the flexible, shining being who flickered about him.

'I am Hermes, messenger of all the gods.'

'What do you want with me?'

'Hera, queen of Heaven, has sent me to fetch you to Olympus.'

The misshapen creature of the grotto scowled till his fierce eyes seemed to withdraw altogether inside the caverns of his head. He limped to his forge and began to work the bellows. The light from the fire cast wild images on his face, so that Hermes fancied that the formidable creature was grinning.

'And if I refuse, Hermes?'

The god of tricks and lies, who had been picking up the various bracelets and marvellous necklaces that littered the forge, sat himself down and looked up at Hephaestus amiably.

'Between you and me, Hephaestus, I wouldn't blame you for deciding to stay here in your comfortable forge with everything to hand and nothing to distract you. But Hera has a husband: Zeus, king of the sky—lord of the gods. And though Zeus is my father, Hephaestus, I would not cross him in anything. His anger might make your forge hotter than you bargain for, my friend. Believe me, I say all this for your own good, Hephaestus. . . .'

Hephaestus hitched aside his leather apron and scratched at his great chest.

'So you are a son of Zeus,' he murmured.

The two gods stared at one another: the subtle god of illusions, quickness and cunning invention—and the slow, lonely god of beauty distilled from anguish and serenity hammered out of pain.

Then Hephaestus smiled wryly round the grotto he had come to love. Briefly his deep eyes twinkled as he saw that

Hermes had stolen a ring, fashioned like a snake, and was endeavouring to conceal it from him. 'Come, brother; let us go.'

'Here is the maker of the brooch, great lady. Here is the god from beneath the sea.' Then Hermes, his limbs still jewelled from the waves, leaped down and hid himself among the bright throng that jostled in the hall.

A monster stood against the sky. Rough, savage, misshapen —his sunken eyes screwed up against the light. His great bulk seemed scarcely supported on his bent, weak legs . . . and he swayed in the casement, while the passing air tugged at his black tufted head.

Instinctively Hera put out a hand to save him from falling—then withdrew it under a sudden piercing gaze. There was no mistaking the eye of a god.

Hephaestus stared at the magnificent goddess in robes of scarlet and black: the queen of Heaven.

A moment he had long awaited.

'Do you still dream of revenge?' Eurynome's words in the grotto echoed yet in his head. Even as he'd mounted through the air with Hermes by his side, those words had boomed and thundered. Well . . . well . . . now the dream had come home to roost.

He peered from god to flawless god. There leaned Poseidon, large and surly; there was Hades by him . . . and Hestia . . . then once more the imperial lady of the sky. She flinched a little as his eyes met hers. Revenge. . . . But she was a little less than the cruel goddess of his dreams; and a little more, besides. The hand she'd put out to save him. . . . He shook his ugly head—and sighed. The revenge that had come home to roost had laid its egg—but he had not the heart to consume it: it was too small.

'Who—are—you, Hephaestus?'

The lady Hera's face was white. Her bosom trembled as the strange monster's eyes searched her through and through.

'I am your son, great Hera. I am the child you cast into the sea. I was ugly then; am I not hideous now?'

The pallor of the goddess's face gave way to a deep red. She could no longer support Hephaestus's gaze. The queen of Heaven bowed her head. Hephaestus scowled. 'Why did you call me here?'

'I did not know. I only saw your work. I had never seen such beauty anywhere in the universe. I marvelled at it—and desired it.'

Her voice was low, uncertain . . . and the misshapen god leaned forward to catch her words. Once more her hand went out as if to steady him; and once more she drew it back under his sharp gaze.

'And now?'

'I am ashamed, Hephaestus.'

The goddess's voice was suddenly firm, even cold. And her head was high.

'The hand you stretched out, great Hera—'

'Yes?'

'May I see it again?'

The goddess lifted her white arm.

'Was this the hand that cast me out?'

'Yes.'

Revenge . . . revenge . . . the scrawny bird screeched and twittered in Hephaestus's savage head.

'I had not dreamed it was so beautiful.' He still scowled—but it was against the prickling radiance in the hall. 'If it is still your wish, great lady, I will make you bracelets for this arm and rings for these fingers such as will be the envy of creation.'

Then Hephaestus held out his own scorched and twisted hand with its immensely strong fingers. Briefly it nested in the great goddess's white palm. Her fingers closed upon it and the monstrous son felt his mother's strength gently drawing him down into the chamber.

His weak legs stumbled as he touched the floor—then all the silent multitude gave a mighty shout.

'Welcome, Hephaestus, maker of beauty! Welcome, great god of the hammer and fire!'

So . . . so, he was on Olympus at last. Well he supposed one might grow used to it. One grew used to anything, in time —even a grotto under the sea.

He moved among the gleaming throng, seeing with his own aching eyes the gods he'd heard of only, had seemed to invent inside his head. They were different . . . curiously different. Hestia was warmer, gentler than he'd supposed, while great Demeter was more generous in her dimensions and wore a soft, wide, amorous smile.

Well, well: the immortal gods—

He saw the Titan Prometheus standing somewhat apart; and, strangely, that vast being was greater than he'd dreamed—more haunted of eye and deeper of purpose.

Radiance . . . radiance everywhere; his poor eyes found no shadows, no rest.

His glittering mother was offering him a forge with twenty giant bellows and all the gold he could work. Well, well—his were busy hands and they longed to be a-making. He nodded and shuffled on, peering sideways, half-grinning, half-scowling, and mumbling under his breath.

Then he came to his father, almighty Zeus; and even the lord of the sky was not as he'd supposed. Though the great god's radiance was blinding and his stature immense, Hephaestus felt no fear of him; and when he bowed his head it was only because Zeus's brightness hurt his eyes.

'You shall make me thunderbolts,' said the father of the gods. 'And Olympus will never fall.'

Wearily Hephaestus nodded, and his father smiled. 'I see you carry your birthright in your hands, my ugly son—and in your skilful head. What then will you ask of me as a father's gift?'

Gift . . . gift? What did he want that he could not make? He looked about him. His dreams had been so different.

Then suddenly he saw one that was not. Once, he remembered, he had dreamed of a nymph that answered all his desires. She was compounded of many images and many aspects of them. She was such a nymph as only writhed and moaned and lay amid the pillows of the mind. So he had made her—as best he could—in blushing coral.

But now he saw her, laughing and moving in the hall. His nymph—at last a dream was answered and Olympus had been worth the ascent.

'Give me *her*,' muttered Hephaestus—and pointed to Aphrodite.

The hall fell silent. Aphrodite's doves and sparrows flickered uncertainly about her golden head; and Athene's owl, freed from its pain and misery, opened wide its timeless orange eyes.

'Give me my nymph.'

Aphrodite, her laughter stifled, looked uncertainly at mighty Zeus. The great god stared at his deformed son and then at the magical goddess of desire. He frowned at the terrible inequality of the match.

'Ask again, Hephaestus—'

'Does great Zeus deny his first-born son a gift?' said Hera coldly. 'Or does he seek Aphrodite for himself?'

Zeus's frown grew dark as thunder—and the throng in the hall began to dwindle before the coming storm.

'What right has he by Aphrodite's side?'

'A better right than you, lord Zeus.'

'Hera—'

'All the gods are witness to it. You offered a gift; then denied it.'

'Hera—'

But the queen of Heaven was not dismayed by Zeus's mounting anger. Her own overtopped it. She stood opposing him and her splendid eyes flashed with fury for her son.

'So . . . so . . .' said Zeus, at length. 'The gift. Since I promised and your mother wishes it, take Aphrodite for your wife.' The great god nodded in confirmation of his word, and thunder was in the air.

Then Hephaestus took her—this most marvellous creation of Zeus's—and walked the length of the hall with her, his seamed and ugly head scarce reaching to her matchless shoulder. Her doves and sparrows tried to peck him, but he drove them off with a wave of his vast dark hand. He grinned and grinned; and frightened Aphrodite, in spite of herself, began to laugh again.

Then they left the hall, led by triumphant Hera; and the banquet guests followed uneasily after.

Zeus remained behind. His brow was black as night. Had there been thunderbolts to hand, Olympus would have rocked to them.

Suddenly he was not alone. In the midst of the vast golden floor, whining with hatred and infantile rage, crouched little Ares.

'My gift—my gift!' he screamed, and beat the floor with his fists. 'The nymph was mine! Father Zeus—you've cheated me! You've given me no birthright! What can I be god of?'

Mighty Zeus stared down at the child who was as misshapen within as was his brother without.

'Hatred! Discord! War!' shouted the lord of the sky. 'Let that be your birthright, Ares! What else are you fit for?'

Then he rose and left the hall in a blaze that seared the infant's eyes.

For a little while, the child whimpered alone; and then, as if wafted through a keyhole, came crooked-smiling Hermes.

'Poor Ares—and on your birthday, too!'

'The earth—the earth!' shouted the child suddenly, and ran to the casement that overlooked the pleasant world. 'I want the earth!'

Hermes joined him and looked down.

'They say the earth is for none of us. Not even for you, Ares.'

'Then who will have it? Tell me and I'll tear him to pieces!'

Hermes glanced at the raging child, and even he was chilled as little Ares swore the oath that the gods must never break.

'I swear by the River Styx that whoever has the earth I will tear and bite and hack into bloody pieces! I swear—I swear!'

The earth—the sweet green earth. To whom would it be given? Hermes brooded—then bethought himself of the Muses on Mount Parnassus. From them he was to learn the secrets of prophecy and all that was to come.

He climbed up on to the casement and, with a brief backward look at savage Ares, he flew outward like a mighty silver bird, and winged his way towards Parnassus.

PART II

●

THE MAKING OF MEN

8● The Creatures of Prometheus

Three blind, stone-faced beings crouched in the groin of a mountain. Robed in white, they were neither nymphs nor goddesses nor the daughters of anything that had ever seen the light of day. From time to time, their thin arms and sharp fingers would reach out to fondle certain curious objects that were placed in their midst. A spinning-wheel, a measuring rod—and a pair of shears. A short way below there grew an ancient thornbush against which the mountain goats would brush and leave clots of their hair. Whenever this happened, one of the blind three would rise and stumble to the bush, finger it over for wool and return to her sisters with her gleanings, which she would add to an already sizeable pile.

Their names were as strange as their occupation. Clotho, the spinner; Lachesis, the measurer; and, smallest yet most terrible, Atropos—she who cannot be avoided—the wielder of the shears.

They were the Fates. . . .

Suddenly, they turned their blind faces upward; and their sockets, half-grown over, resembled irregular black stars in their heads.

Said Clotho, 'A sudden brightness passed. At great speed—and very high. I felt it, sisters. . . .'

'It was a god,' mumbled Lachesis. 'I know the warmth and the scent of them. It was a god flying from Olympus towards Parnassus. He will be there by now. . . .'

Then shrunken Atropos, forever playing with her shears, said shrilly: 'It was Hermes, sisters, it is the day we have waited for. Listen—listen—'

The three creatures bent their heads towards each other, and began to smile. A faint but unmistakable creaking sound was

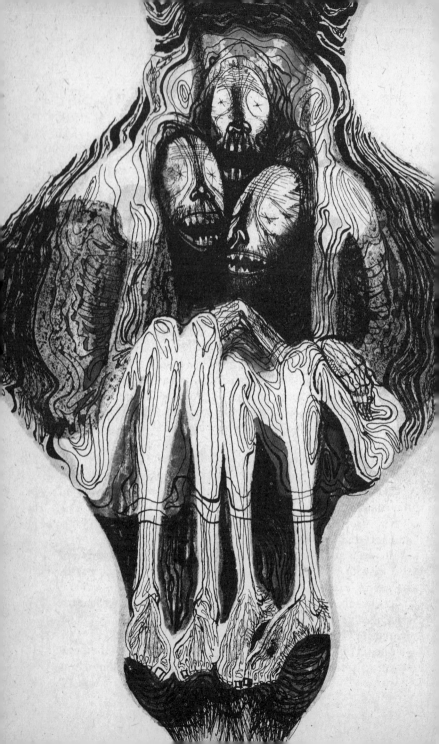

heard; the wheel had begun to turn.

The dreadful hands of Clotho and Lachesis reached out; and Atropos's fingers tightened over her shears.

Far, far aloft, immortal Hermes brushed a fold of cloud aside and looked down.

He saw the three white shrouded sisters sitting like maggots in the mountain's groin. Many times he had seen them before; but now there was a difference.

Their spinning wheel was moving; and the three sisters had leaned forward as if they were about to begin—what?

Hermes frowned—and sped even faster to Parnassus where all answers were to be learned.

He reached the mountain where the three grave Muses instructed the wild children of the wild nymphs. Once, these daughters of Zeus had been wild themselves, but time, responsibility and the dignified example of Apollo had mellowed them into three goddesses as wise as they were respectable.

They drew their robes about them at the god's approach, endeavouring to conceal their beautiful limbs from the bright fire of his gaze. But Hermes was most studiously polite, and the gleam that had risen to the eyes of the once wild sisters died slowly away.

Augury . . . prophecy . . . the future. He had understood from his friend and brother Apollo that he might learn it on Parnassus.

The Muses stared at the youthful god who stood so straight and bright in their quiet glade. So . . . so he had only come to learn. They sighed, recalling, perhaps, their old days; then they led him to a stone basin filled with mountain water and showed him how to cast five white pebbles sideways into it.

'You must watch the way they dance, sweet Hermes. And mark how they fall. It is all in the pattern of their movement and the design of their rest. See . . . see. . . .'

They cast the pebbles, splashing one another as they did so— and gently shrieking; then inadvertently splashing the god and hastening to dry his fair limbs on their gowns. . . . 'See . . . see . . . like so!'

Hermes smiled—and learned.

Then they left him, for the god had caught the skill with

wonderful speed.

They glanced back through the trees and saw him crouching over the stone basin with the pebbles held in his cupped hands.

He shook them, whispered to them, shook them again. 'Who will inherit the earth?'

Then he cast them sideways into the water and watched them dance and fall.

What was their answer? Slowly, Hermes read it out. 'It—concerns—Prometheus.'

The god frowned in surprise. Again he shook the pebbles, whispered and cast them into the basin. 'Why has Clotho's wheel begun to turn? What is she to spin? What will Lachesis measure—and what will Atropos cut?'

The pebbles rattled against the stone sides like frightened fishes; then they came to rest. 'It—concerns—Prometheus.'

Again Hermes frowned; and for a third time shook the pebbles, whispered to them and hissed them on their way.

'When will this be?'

The pebbles dropped, rolled a little, then were still. Their answer was, '*Even now.*'

Prometheus had a garden in Attica; a pleasant, cultivated grove in the lap of Mount Hymettus where the wild bees made the honey from which the nymphs distilled the nectar for the gods. Here, the Titan and his brother grew such fruits as the earth would yield and had built themselves a house round an ancient fig-tree. It had been Hestia herself who had taught them the art of building; and wise Athene had come often to sit and talk of how best to cultivate the soil while her beloved owl had perched in the wrinkled branches of the tree.

But now the Titans walked among their glades and across their close-cut lawns. Prometheus was troubled; his mighty head was bowed in thought. He feared for the lovely earth.

Little by little the brothers' shadows lengthened as the sun rode down into the sea. Prometheus was silent and Epithemeus, his brother, shrugged his shoulders and returned into the house. Of the two, he was the simpler and did not foresee, as Prometheus did, that present pleasure may be bought too dear.

Prometheus stared through the shadowy leaves of his orchards to the wide expanse beyond.

'All this,' he whispered, 'to no purpose? It cannot be!'

He raised his unhappy eyes and gazed towards Olympus. He tried to fathom what might be in the mind of almighty Zeus. He did not trust the god. He believed that sooner or later Zeus would beget a child and give it the world to play with. Even a child like murderous Ares. . . .

He shivered and knelt down. He took up a handful of the rich earth and crushed it in his fist. He opened his hand. The earth, moist from the rain, had taken the imprint of his fingers. He frowned and tried to mould it further, thinking of the marvellous coral nymph the ugly Hephaestus had made under the sea. But he lacked the god's skill and his effort was vague and clumsy. Must the Olympians always be better than he? Angrily he threw it down and stode on to where a stream whispered lazily among tall reeds. Here the soil was heavy with clay and more obedient to the shaping hand. So Prometheus made a second image; and it looked like a little angry Zeus.

Prometheus laughed; then, suddenly, a strange excitement filled him.

He bent down and with both his vast hands gathered up more clay. He scooped out half the bed of the stream, so that the worried waters gushed and gurgled as if in a whirlpool.

Then, when the moon was gone into a cloud and the garden was in darkness, he hastened back to his home with the clay still dripping in his arms. He believed he had been very secret.

There was a room in the Titans' home that belonged to Prometheus alone. Its rafters were formed from the trimmed and polished branches of the fig-tree that still grew from the middle of the floor. It was in this room that Athene had loved to sit and discourse with the profound Titan on matters of the universe, while aloft her owl made two orange suns with its eyes.

The room was rich and heavy with thought. It was here that Prometheus brought the clay and laid it on an oiled and polished bench that stretched for the room's great length.

Under this bench were several stone jars, well stoppered and sealed. No one knew of these jars but the two Titans who had guarded them jealously since the far-off days of murdered Uranus. One of them was cracked and skilfully repaired. The damage had been done during the wild war between the Titans and the gods. A mountain had crashed to blazing ruin and shaken the jar from a shelf. But Prometheus had saved it.

Now at last he broke the seal and opened it. Within was the divine substance of Chaos from which all things had been created.

Prometheus had seen it, still ungrown, lying in a deep pit. It had glimmered and winked up at him. Eagerly he'd gathered it and stored it in the jars.

He poured it out. Everywhere in its shining bulk were the bright, immortal seeds trapped like fireflies in some black, festooning web.

Firmly and quickly the great Titan kneaded this ancient substance into the riverbed clay, till the precious seeds were evenly distributed. Then he set to work in earnest.

In the groin of the Fates' mountain the three blind sisters laughed aloud. Their wheel was creaking and grunting as it spun like a mad thing.

Prometheus shaped the clay into images of the immortal gods. His fingers grew more and more skilful as his great mind wrestled with the mysterious quest for form. His memory and imagination seemed to body forth shapes in the air, and swiftly he enclosed them in the curious clay.

Little Zeuses, Heras, Apollos and Poseidons ran from his finger-tips; even a dark-browed Hades and a proud Artemis with a wart on her knee where the Titan's finger had fumbled.

Then he set the little godkins up before him and rested his mighty head on his aching hands. Already the immortal seeds had begun to stir and grow within the thick insensitive clay. Quietly, the Titan watched.

But he was not the only watcher. High among the crooked rafters perched an intent bird. It was a crane whose bright, bright eyes were the eyes of Hermes. . . .

The clay was swelling, growing. Channels were being formed within it down which the burst seeds sent crimson tears to course, nourishing, colouring and warming into life.

Eyelids grew thin as gauze, flicked open to reveal strange little pools of wonderment. Lips reddened, parted on white teeth . . . and tongues began to stir under the force of mounting breath.

And still they grew till their proportions were all but godlike. Everywhere in the vast room limbs were stretching, bodies twisting and hair stirring in the night breeze.

At last, they grew no more. The seeds had spent themselves; their task was done. The great Titan smiled.

'Go,' he whispered. 'Go seek your inheritance before it is too late.'

His door was open and the starlight drifting in glinted on their sweet new limbs.

They turned their faces back to the vast dark room in which they had been made. Their eyes met the deep eyes of Prometheus. They smiled—and then they went out into the glorious garden of the night.

The Titan watched them and inexplicably his eyes grew full of tears and his huge heart ached with love and hope for the creatures he had made.

Suddenly, one gave a wild, wild cry and fell at the foot of a poplar tree. Prometheus hastened to his side; stared down, touched—then recoiled. His new-made child was cold and still.

In the groin of the gaunt mountain the three blind, stone-faced creatures laughed again. Atropos fingered her shears. The blades were sharp. To test them—just to test them—she had slit a new-spun thread.

Prometheus knelt beside his cold, quiet creation, not instantly knowing what was amiss, what had fled.

The watchful crane that had perched in the rafters was gone. Hermes the messenger had taken a shade to the echoing world of the dead. Alone and bewildered, it flitted on the further bank of the River Styx.

The first man had died.

'So frail a thread?' whispered Prometheus. 'Was it the clay . . . or the seeds themselves? I had hoped—but it was not to be. What can you do against the gods and the Fates with the fragile, pitiful life I've given you?'

Then Prometheus buried his dead in the shadow of the poplar tree and mourned till it was light.

9 ● Fire

'My father bids me tell you to destroy them, great Prometheus; or he will do so himself.'

Thus Hermes, messenger of the gods, as he stood, piercing bright, in the Titan's garden, washed by the morning sun.

'Why? Why? How have they offended? What is their crime?'

'Who knows what is in the mind of Zeus? Perhaps he is offended, Lord Prometheus? Perhaps he finds what you have made too close in aspect to the gods? Perhaps he sees them as a mockery? Gods who are subject to the Fates. . . . Destroy them, Prometheus. So my father says.'

'And you, good Hermes? Is it your wish, too?'

The god looked sideways, avoiding the Titan's despairing eyes; shifted from foot to winged foot and smiled as his shadow seemed to dance off into the trees.

'Between you and me, Prometheus . . . no. Not particularly, that is. I think they have a certain charm. Personally, I like them. I assure you, Prometheus, that such messages as, from time to time, I bring from this great god or that, do not necessarily reflect my own opinions.'

Hermes, ever politic, ever unwilling to offend, watched the mighty Titan curiously; he continued, 'Believe me, my friend —I understand your affection and your sorrow. When I summoned the shade of the one that died, I was troubled, Prometheus. As we entered the grove of black poplars, this shade and I, it asked me: Why, why? And I could not answer. Then, when I led it to the dark river and dragged it aboard the evil, rotting boat, and it saw there was no one else there but bony Charon, again it begged me: Why, why?

'We came to the further bank, and still there was no one else by. And so to the Field of Asphodel: empty, empty. . . .

'It clung to me, Prometheus, as I left it, still begging me to tell it why.

'It knew nothing; had not lived more than the winking of an eye—yet it sensed the vastness of its loss. I looked back, and never in all the universe have I seen anything so lonely as that single, frightened shade wandering over the ashy ground and crying: Why, why?'

The Titan listened and groaned in anguish; then Hermes added softly: 'They are so frail, Prometheus. Your creatures are so pitifully frail. Are they worth their labour?'

Eagerly the Titan laid his hand on Hermes' ribboned staff—as if to deflect or soften the god's terrible message.

'But I will strengthen them! I will refine the substance, purify it and pluck out the seeds that menace. I—'

'It is too late, Prometheus. They are doomed.'

'By Zeus?'

'If not by my father, then by every wind that blows. How could they endure, never knowing when Atropos might take it into her blind head to slit the thread of their lives?'

How indeed? And the more Hermes argued, the more intolerable seemed the burden Prometheus' fragile creatures would have to bear.

Yet their very frailty stung the Titan's heart and strengthened his great will. He begged bright Hermes to plead with his father for a little respite. If the creatures were destined to flicker out—then let them perish of their own accord. But spare them the dreadful thunderbolt. Let them see and love the gods, however briefly, and, maybe, find some favour in their sight—

Here, subtle Hermes pursed his lips and tapped his staff against his head.

'Between you and me, my friend, I fancy you've hit on something. I don't promise—I never promise—but if your creatures were to find favour in great Zeus's eyes . . . that is to say, if they were to go out of their way to please, then who knows? Think on that, Lord Prometheus; and I will undertake to delay my father's hand.'

Between Arcadia and Attica, there was a place called Sicyon where the creatures of Prometheus had begun to make a home.

It was here, in a myrtle grove—once dear to Hermes—that Prometheus put it into men's minds to honour the gods. A rich, red bull, sleek and portly, was sacrificed and the Titan cupped his hands to his vast mouth and shouted up to Olympus for almighty Zeus to descend and be mankind's first guest.

'See, great god! My creatures honour you and worship you! Come down so they may behold you and give you the best of the earth!'

He shaded his eyes and stared desperately up towards the curtains of cloud that veiled the mountain's divine summit.

Even as he watched, a finger of lightning crooked round them and drew them briefly apart. Then came a roll of thunder. The god had heard. The god would come.

Eagerly Prometheus stripped the blood-dappled skin from the bull and divided the carcass, laying the bones and fat beneath one part of the hide, and the steaming flesh beneath the other; but in his haste he had not detached the stomach. . . . Two portions: one for the god—and one for mankind.

Wide-eyed and innocent that they were, poised on the edge of extinction, the Titan's creatures watched as their great creator toiled and struggled to save them.

Suddenly they shrank back. A fearful radiance seared their naked eyes and scorched their skin. They cried out and fled into the shadows of the myrtles, hiding their faces in their hands. The blaze had been unendurable. It lingered on the inner eye where it burned its vision. Within the scalding radiance had been a shape. A shimmering fluent shape, part man-like, part immeasurably greater. Eyes had seen them— eyes like merciless suns.

It had been the god. . . .

'Welcome, mighty Zeus. Welcome, father of the gods, lord of the sky! Your feast is ready. Mankind awaits.'

The Titan stood back as the fiery god stared round the grove. Then, seeing that Prometheus' poor creatures were blasted by his light, Zeus veiled his lustre and smiled.

He saw the covered portions of the slaughtered bull. He nodded. They had not skimped their offering. The beast had been of the finest.

He touched one portion, lifted a corner of the hide. The

stomach: it reeked of offal. He turned to the other. He glimpsed rich fat. Prometheus trembled; all-seeing Zeus nodded.

He pointed to the second portion.

'I have chosen,' the mighty god decreed. 'From now through all eternity, in feast and holy sacrifice, this portion is for the immortal gods, and that for mankind.'

He flung back the skin he had chosen. Beneath the rich layer of fat lay nothing but the animal's wretched, meatless bones. The divine portion. . . .

Prometheus bowed his head to hide a helpless smile. He awaited the enraged god's thunderbolt. But Zeus' anger took a subtler form.

'Let them eat their flesh raw,' he said. 'I forbid them the use of fire.'

Without fire, they would die. Their slender limbs would freeze, their blood congeal and their bright eyes glaze and film like scum on a quiet pond. The angry god had doomed them as surely as if he'd hurled his thunderbolt and scorched them in an instant.

Prometheus wept slow, bitter tears. It had been his own smile that had brought it about: mighty Zeus had taken this way of punishing him. The smile of the father was to be the death's-head grin of his children.

For a while, fury took hold of him—and his gentle brother watched with terror and awe as great Prometheus paced their garden, bursting asunder the well-tended trees as if they'd been straw. Then the Titan passed into despair. War and violence had ever been hateful to him. The mighty struggles his nature demanded had all been in the mind.

He knew he could not storm Olympus and drag down the father of the gods. He lacked both Zeus' strength and Zeus' instant passion. Thinking had ever held him back.

For long it had preserved him—and saved him from the fearful fate of all his race. But now that power had reached its end—the limits of his mind. Thought stared into soul; and soul stared back at thought. They were the same; and the tragic Titan knew that he must destroy himself to save his children: men.

Some time during the night, mankind saw him shining among the thick trees that cloaked the northern slopes of Mount Olympus. His light pierced the branches so that it seemed as if some star had fallen and been caught in a vast black net.

Then his light was snuffed in a deep cleft in the rock, and the Titan mounted unseen.

An owl flew out of the trees, screeched several times, then fluttered uncertainly, hovering as if seeking its moment to pounce. It screeched again, and began to pursue a devious path in the night air, leading higher and higher up the mountain.

It was the owl of the goddess Athene.

The hidden Titan saw it and knew that the goddess had not turned against him. She had sent her owl to lead him secretly into the fortress of the gods. This was the most she could do for him. Mighty though she was, even she feared her blazing father's wrath.

Now came another bird out of the night. A crane perched in the Titan's twisting path. It stared at him with bright, inquisitive eyes.

'Though I will not help you, Prometheus,' whispered the voice of cunning Hermes, 'I will not stand in your path.' The crane flew off and its soft cry came back to the mounting Titan. 'There is what you seek in my brother Hephaestus' forge.'

Flames gleamed and danced on the twenty golden bellows as they rose and fell like twenty gigantic beating hearts. They breathed on the forge, increasing its fire till the lip of its rocky prison shivered and ran.

Shadows loomed and lumbered against the huge smithy's walls. Rods and crucibles made the shapes of nodding beasts; and in their midst crouched the shadow of a misshapen monster on bird-thin legs that were broken sharply by the angle of the floor and walls. Hephaestus was at work. He was making a wedding gift for Aphrodite, his wife. He scowled tempestuously as he beat out the gold on the black anvil with a loud, regular clang. He was fashioning the clasp of a girdle. . . .

Suddenly the god's heat-inflamed eyes quickened. A strange shadow had crossed his on the wall. It moved secretly among the beast-like shadows of the rods and crucibles which seemed to nod and swear at it, then crowd it under their own dangerous night.

Hephaestus turned. He saw a hand, holding an unkindled torch. He saw it reach forward, plunge in and out of the fire. The torch flared. It was alight.

The god looked up. Prometheus stood before him.

'For my children,' whispered the despairing Titan. 'For mankind.'

The two great outcasts stared at one another.

'Take it and be gone,' muttered the god.

For long after the Titan had departed, Hephaestus brooded over his anvil. His mighty hammer leaned against his knee . . . and the beaten gold grew cool. Then the god began again. His hammer rose and fell till fountains of sparks leaped up and seemed to engulf him in robes of broken fire.

At last he rested. The smithy grew quiet and the ugly god examined the clasp he had made. It was a golden hand holding a torch. It seemed to be caressing it, and the torch was spurting its vital fire. So delicately wrought was this hand that it seemed to tremble—to move, even with tenderness. . . .

The god nodded. Here in this eternal clasp was his own fierce love for Aphrodite—and Prometheus' aching love for mankind.

He fastened it to the girdle with rivets as fine as hair and hobbled off to the laughing goddess of his dreams.

10 ● An Ordinary Woman

Still Zeus did not strike the defiant Titan down. Prometheus had opposed him, set his command aside. Fire flickered below and strengthened the new, aspiring life.

Time and again Prometheus turned his eyes to heaven so that he might see his destruction blazing forth. But the lord of the sky seemed to have turned his back. Had grave Athene pleaded with her father? Had subtle Hermes put a case?

The Titan's uncertainty grew agonised as his time ran out. Nonetheless, he still laboured for his creatures, teaching them what he could to widen their narrow foothold between the Fates and the gods. At night he brooded in the mysterious room where man had been born. Already he had begun to refine the precious substance of Chaos. Strange spots and scales he'd discovered on the bright seeds. These he scraped away and confined in a small jar which he sealed and hid. He suspected them to be some malignant rot. . . .

'Can you fashion a woman, my clever, ugly son? Can you make her as skilfully as Prometheus made his creatures below?'

The father of the gods stared down from his gold and ivory throne in the great council chamber. 'Not of gold, nor silver, nor imperishable bronze; but of the self-same clay the Titan used—the soft wet clay of Attica?'

Hephaestus shuffled and blinked his reddened eyes away from Zeus' radiance. The fire of his forge was as night beside the blazing noon of Zeus.

'Fetch me the clay and I will make such a woman.'

Zeus nodded; and swift as thought Hermes sped down, twisting through the cloudy swarms of bees that sang above the lower slopes of Mount Hymettus.

Hephaetus waited; and presently, the thieving god returned with Prometheus' clay.

Hephaestus set about his task and Hermes, leaning against the lintel post of the smithy door, watched the great artificer at his work.

Unlike Prometheus, the god worked slowly, He seemed to seek the form within the dull shapeless clay. Even as Hermes watched, his burnt and twisted fingers probed and dragged at hair, cheeks, lips, breasts and limbs as if he was freeing rather than creating them. He tore the clay away from her eyes as if it had been a blindfold; and suddenly a woman stared at Hermes in the doorway. Even though he knew his ill-tempered brother's marvellous skill, Hermes was startled by this strange new evidence of it.

Her height was perhaps a finger's breadth below Aphrodite's; but otherwise her beauty was not of Olympus. It had the darker, richer colours of the earth. Hephaestus had fashioned a woman far beyond the Titan's skill.

She stood beside the mighty anvil and as the twenty golden bellows breathed on the fire, the heat drew tears of moisture out of the clay so that she seemed to be weeping before she had life. Then Zeus bade Aeolus, warder of the four winds, breathe life into her nostrils and mouth.

She stirred; she moved; she stared about her with a sweet vacancy, understanding nothing—feeling nothing.

Being formed from unseeded clay, she had neither passions nor qualities.

So life-giving Zeus commanded the immortal gods to enrich her with their gifts.

First Hestia, gentlest of the children of Cronus, gave this woman a gentleness and generosity not unlike her own; and the vacant eyes took on a soft and tender gleam. But Ares, roughly elbowing forward, forced on her a touch of himself, so that behind the tender gleam there glinted the flicker of a savage fire.

Next great Apollo gave her sweet and tempting grace of movement—such as he himself delighted in; but straightway his moon-sister Artemis gave her defensive quickness, modesty and virginity.

Glorious Demeter shook her head. Never quite in sympathy

with Artemis, she blessed the woman with a richly fertile womb—and the knowledge of it. This knowledge now glinted mysteriously from under the downcast lashes that the mighty huntress's gift had imposed.

'And I will give her wisdom,' said Athene suddenly. She had divined the danger there lurked in this woman, compounded as she was of so many opposing passions. 'I will give her wisdom so that her gifts may be well-used.'

Zeus frowned; but could not deny the powerful goddess her right. So he bade Hermes give Athene's gift a double edge, with curiosity and deceit.

Now the woman turned and smiled gratefully at each of the gods in turn; her eyes seemed to linger so that her last look was always sideways . . . till imperious Hera hastened to cover her nakedness with fine, cloudy robes. This woman was curiously disturbing. Beside her, the hot numphs were but as children—their amorous leapings and twinings as children's games. . . . Then Zeus gave her a name: Pandora—all giving.

She bowed her head. 'Great goddess,' she murmured, raising her face now to lovely Aphrodite while her eyes lingered timidly on smiling Zeus. 'Is there no gift from you? Are you displeased with me? Have I unknowingly offended you? If so, I beg forgiveness . . . and plead for your gift. For without it, I think, all would wither away unused.'

So Aphrodite laughed—and lent Pandora the girdle that Hephaestus had made for her—the girdle that kindled desire.

'With such a piece of work,' murmured the king of the gods as he brooded down on Pandora, 'what need have I of thunderbolts?'

It was Hermes who led her down the slopes of Mount Olympus; and as the gods watched, none was sorry to see her go.

'What harsh message do you bring from Olympus now, Hermes?'

Prometheus and his brother were in their orchard, securing the well-filled branches with stout props, when the great herald rippled through the trees.

'No message, Lord Prometheus,' answered the god courteously. He had plucked an apple in passing and now speared it idly on his ribboned staff. He stared at it as if surprised. 'I bring a gift. Indeed, Prometheus, there is no need to look at me so angrily, as if you would refuse. The gift does not concern you. It is for your brother, Epimetheus.'

He pointed his staff, with the red apple on its head, at the second Titan, the ever-gentle, not over-wise Epimetheus.

'The gift of the gods is for you.'

Epimetheus came forward with a pleased smile. His heart was open; his nature unsuspecting. Such happy beings as he are always the last of their race.

'Beware of gods bearing gifts,' muttered his great brother whom he never understood.

Epimetheus looked uncertain. Hermes stretched out his staff. 'Come,' he called. 'Pandora!'

She came from behind the trees in the cloudy gown of Hera. She walked with graceful yet uncertain steps. Her eyes were downcast—though from time to time they glimmered with a curious sideways glance that lingered in Epimetheus' heart

'Here is your new gift, Epimetheus. Pandora—gift of the Olympian gods.'

Epimetheus was entranced. Never had their orchard seen a richer fruit.

'Beware, brother—'

'Lord Prometheus, this is no concern of yours.' Hermes spoke calmly, but there was an edge to his voice. Then he laughed disarmingly. 'Epimetheus—your deep brother is too anxious. He mistrusts good fortune. Between you and me, I suspect a little envy. And who could blame him? See—'

He touched the trembling Pandora with his staff, laying its appled tip on her breast. She smiled timidly. 'She bears the gifts of us all.'

'She is the gift of Zeus, brother. Old Cronus once had such a gift. Do you remember a cup of honied drink—?'

Epimetheus hesitated; gazed uneasily from brother to the god. He avoided Pandora's eyes. He thanked Olympus, but begged time to consider. . . .

Prometheus smiled triumphantly.

'Do you refuse me, Epimetheus?' Pandora's voice was low . . . even pleading. The gentle Titan glanced at her. Modestly she cast her eyes down to Aphrodite's kindling girdle. Epimetheus felt desire rise like the all-covering sea.

Then briefly Pandora lifted her eyes and stared at Prometheus. Her look was still gentle and partly timid. She seemed to be bewildered and curious as to why this mighty being should bid his brother send her away. What had she done? Why did he stare at her as if to pierce her through and through? Why did his great brows furrow till his eyes were no more than pools of troubled shadow? Was it only because she had come between brother and brother? Was it as the bright god had said—that this vast soul was stabbed with envy for his brother's blessing?

If so, then it was not of her doing. . . .

See—he was drawing Epimetheus aside, talking with him—while the god who had brought her looked on with the strangest smile. What was to become of her, with all her beauty and gifts?

Why had the gods made her so?

'Do not refuse me, Epimetheus,' she pleaded; and such was her power that Epimetheus' heart faltered within him. She promised him such joy and fierce delight that even the gods would envy him. Epimetheus' eyes began to gleam. Whereupon the blessing of Hestia, momentarily conquering the passions of Aphrodite and Ares, prompted Pandora to speak of ease and sweet companionship, and the speaking silences of harmonious kinds. . . .

'Can there be danger in such a gift?' asked simple Epimetheus of his brother.

'Nor will their lives be fruitless, Lord Prometheus,' murmured Hermes, drifting close and leaning towards the Titan's ear. 'Glorious Demeter has blessed her, too. Even as your well-tended trees bear fine fruit, so will Pandora bear children to your home. Mark my words, Prometheus, her children will inherit our immortal gifts—for the gods' gifts do not die—and these children will mingle with mankind. Thus does my father mean well, Prometheus. He seeks to improve on your charming but fragile creation with some more durable qualities of the gods. Believe me, my friend—'

Suddenly the Titan turned with terror on the murmuring god of lies. His eyes were wild—his vast comprehension tilted so that all ran down into the pit of dismay. He had divined dread Zeus' purpose—and foreseen his own defeat. The

creatures that he loved—the creatures who might have inherited the earth as neither gods nor Titans were permitted
to do—were to be crippled before they had begun.

Even as in Pandora the passions of the gods opposed each
other, so they would in men. All aspiration would be lamed,
all achievement warped as man eternally fought within himself
a battle that could be neither lost nor won.

The great Titan raised his eyes to Mount Olympus and
cursed immortal Zeus.

He lifted up his voice and hurled his curses till they echoed
in the far corners of the universe. Even in hateful Tartarus they
were heard, like thin, high whispers over the ceaseless weeping
and groaning of the Titans who were chained there.

Close by the dreary Fields of Asphodel, there is a pool
beside which grows a bone-white poplar tree. It is the pool of
memory. Here strayed the solitary shade of the man who had
died. Vainly it drank of the pool; but what memories could it
recapture of a life so fleeting, save an aching glimpse of a
garden by night?

It heard Prometheus' curses and shook its thin head. 'Why?
Why?' it wailed—and flittered away into the lonely gloom.

Grim Hades in his palace heard them—and nodded in
expectation of his vast brother's revenge.

As in a dream, Prometheus saw Hermes flicker away; and with
a last stab of anguish he saw his brother and Pandora retreat
with frightened faces, and run from the orchard. Their hands
had been clasped—and there was no undoing them now.

Prometheus bowed his mighty head. He heard a rushing in
the air. It was coming; and he was almost glad of it—the
thunderbolt of Zeus!

The trees blazed and, for an instant, their blackened branches
reached up like imploring arms with fingers charred and
flaming.

A radiance that seared even the Titan's ancient eyes stood
in the ruined orchard like a fiery sword. Zeus in all his unendurable glory was come for his revenge.

Far, far to the north, amid the freezing mountains of the
Caucasus, there stood a tall, cold pillar. Chains of unburstable

iron hung from its base and capital. Here the naked Titan was manacled by wrists and ankles, stretched so that he could scarcely twist his body or avert his head.

He waited—then a shadow fell across his face. He rolled his eyes to see what had come between him and the pale, bitter sun.

A vulture with hooked talons and greedy beak hung in the air. Its stony eyes met his. Then it swooped and the Titan writhed and screamed till the mountains cracked. His agony had begun. Again and again the hungry bird flew at him and tore at his undefended liver. When night came with biting frosts and whirling snow, the Titan's wounds healed and he grew whole again. But when the cold sun rose, the self-same shadow fell across his face and the Titan waited for his agony to begin once more. Such was the punishment of Prometheus, maker of men.

Epimetheus, the last of the Titans, wept for his mighty brother —whom he had never understood. In his great sadness Pandora comforted him, and little by little, Epimetheus began to think his brother had misjudged her. She was so quick to understand and minister to his every need. She never crossed nor questioned him; nor did she plead to enter his lost brother's mysterious room. For Prometheus, in his last moments of liberty, had charged his brother most urgently never to enter it or disturb what was hidden there.

Pandora nodded. Though she had not liked Prometheus, she was sensible of her husband's affection and was anxious for him to feel that she was of a like mind. For a while it seemed that the gifts of Hestia and Athene were uppermost.

Then, thanks to the rich soil of Attica, the black scars in the orchard healed over, and the reason for the great Titan's fall faded from Pandora's mind. More and more she came round to the view that the whole unlucky affair had blown up out of jealousy. Why else had her husband's brother so taken against her?

She gazed at her reflection in a pool. Certainly she was beautiful enough to stir envy in any one. After all, the gods had made her. She sighed. It had been tragic; but jealousy was an evil passion and Prometheus had paid for it. She only hoped it would serve as a lesson.

She stood up and thoughts of Prometheus slid into thoughts of the forbidden room. What was so particular about it? She suspected jealousy was at the root of it again. A jealous spirit is jealous in everything. Most likely the room was very handsome and Prometheus had forbidden it to her out of spite. The more she thought of it, the more she was convinced. It irritated her like a crumb in her bed. Wherever she turned for comfort, there it was, scratching away. Agitatedly she left the garden and entered the house. She paced the hall, pausing each time before the closed door. It was ridiculous. She felt she couldn't call her home her own. She laid her hand on the engraved bolt. Epimetheus would get over it. Naturally he'd be hurt at first and grieve for his brother again. But it would pass and then there'd be nothing to come between them. A shadow would have been removed. . . .

Pandora nodded. All in all, it would be for the best. She opened the door.

As she'd suspected, the room was the best in the house. A little dark, perhaps, and certainly dusty . . . but the fig-tree and its polished branches gave it great character and atmosphere.

She ran her finger along the wide bench that stretched from wall to wall. Idly she drew the shape of a baby in the dust. She smiled. The room would make a fine nursery. . . .

No sooner had she thought of it than she set to work. She swept and polished and transformed the shadowy room into a shining joy. She cleared out the cupboards of all old stone jars —but did not open them.

Here she respected her husband's wishes; besides, the jars seemed quite useless.

Then, quite by chance, she came upon a smaller one, tucked underneath the bench. She held it up. It was a pretty jar. Cleaned out, it would hold jewels or perfume. . . . She shook her head. No. She would defer to her husband's wish, foolish as it was.

Then she thought of Prometheus. How like him to keep such a jar for himself! What could he possibly want with it now? After all, it wasn't as though she intended to open *all* the jars.

She had her principles and would not have abandoned them

for anything. She was perfectly certain that her husband would come to see it her way. He would admire her for leaving the other jars and so honouring his selfish brother's memory.

She shook the pretty little jar gently. There was something inside. She listened. It gave a dry rattling sound. She shrugged her shoulders. She'd put up with the sacred memory of Prometheus for long enough. She opened the jar.

She screamed; she shrieked; she dropped the jar. Gentle Epimetheus came running to her cries.

There seemed to be a cloud about Pandora: a whirling, malignant veil that glittered with ten thousand furious wings. They seemed to be insects of extraordinary venom and ferocity. They bit and stung and beat against his crouching wife; then they turned on him and he felt their wicked little spears in every part of his body. He cried out:

'Prometheus, Prometheus! What have we done?'

Far in the north a fiercer pain than the vulture's beak stabbed at the chained Titan. From his icy place of punishment he saw what had befallen his children. His deep eyes filled with tears as a more terrible vulture tore at his heart.

Nor did this phantom bird depart with its bloody brother when healing night came. High in the freezing mountains, striped with the purple glaciers of his blood, Prometheus wept. His labours and his fall had been in vain.

The strange spots and scales he had imprisoned in the jar had been malignant indeed. Unhindered by the divine sub-stance from which they'd been scraped, they had grown into hideous little furies. He had seen them fly out of his house in a wicked cloud to sting his helpless children. Madness, vice, old age and crippling sickness had been let out upon the world as a birthright for man.

Prometheus raised his eyes and stared across the world's night. His eyes met those of bitter Atlas; and these two giants who had opposed the gods looked long and deep at each other from their separate high prisons of pain.

'Mankind,' whispered great Prometheus, 'forgive me; I have failed. Better that I never made you . . . for what is there left to you now?'

85

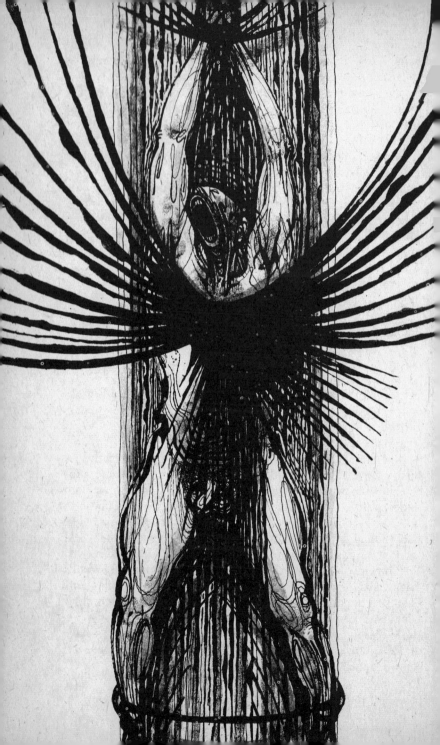

Pandora gazed down at the shattered jar. It was past repairing. She felt awkward. Her husband, inflamed from the strange insects' attacks, had looked at her reproachfully.

So, as mildly as she was able, she remarked that Prometheus was to blame. He should never have kept such things in a jar. She bent down and began to gather the broken pieces. Suddenly she came upon a curious stone. She picked it up. It was not a stone. She looked at it carefully. It seemed to be a chrysalis. . . .

She shivered as she tried to throw it away before it hatched. But it stuck to her fingers.

At last she scraped it off on a fragment of the jar. She rubbed her hands to rid herself of the gum-like substance the chrysalis had left. Her eyes brightened in surprise. The pain of the bites and stings seemed soothed. Eagerly she told Epimetheus. The chrysalis was a balm—a wondrous healing balm.

Pandora was delighted. She smiled at her husband. Was it not a good thing after all that she'd opened the jar? As she'd always told him, everything turned out for the best.

A sudden movement aloft distracted her. She looked up. A bird had been perched in the polished rafters, looking down with bright, inquisitive eyes. It flapped its wings and flew away. It had been a crane. She watched it through the casement as it flew with amazing speed towards the north. It pierced the colder air and crossed the mountains till at last it saw below it the pillar of Prometheus.

'What is there left to mankind now?' cried the despairing Titan as he saw the sideways-dropping god.

'Hope,' answered great Hermes. 'For better or worse—for who knows what may unfold from a chrysalis?—hope was left behind.'

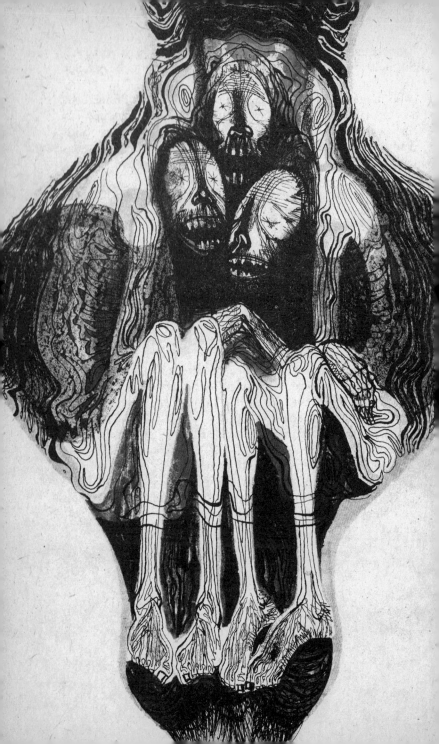

PART III

•

GODS AND MEN

11 ● Wolves

Unchanging Zeus looked down. The glimmering nymphs were harder now to find. The creatures of Prometheus seemed everywhere. Like mice, they filled the shady crannies of the earth. Neither the Fates nor the plagues, nor the loss of their great protector, had extinguished them. They built temples and the soft air was whiskered with the smoke of sacrifices.

They pleased Demeter, who enriched their harvests; and Hestia, who blessed their hearths. All seemed set fair for a second Olympus to be raised on earth. Prometheus had not laboured in vain. He had made man in the image of the immortals—and the gods were flattered to see themselves so dearly imitated.

So the lord of the sky laid aside his blinding fire and thunderbolts and left his palace in the clouds for Arcadia, where once the nymphs had lain thick on the ground. He came at nightfall, in the shape of a humble traveller. . . .

The pinewoods of Lycaeus were dark and full of fumbling shadows. High overhead, the black branches interlocked like giants' fingers over the eye of the moon. But here and there her arrows silvered through and stuck quivering in the ground, their slanting shafts engraved with moss, ferns and misty bark. Unseen animals rustled and padded about their nightly business, briefly pausing as if alarmed by each other's footfalls. . . .

Suddenly, a wind began to blow. Trembling, the animals fled and hid in their lairs as this strange wind came sweeping through the woods from the north. Even the arrows of the moon bent aside for it. . . . Then it passed out of the trees where they gave way to what seemed to be a second forest made of marble.

The palace of Lycaon, king of Arcadia, lay under the moon as proud and silver-white as a city of the gods. Courtyards and colonnaded walls surrounded it, and their shadows stretched like black dreams across a silver world. From time to time, these shadows jumped and divided as light from the palace leaped up . . . most likely when some log was thrown on the hearth or roasting fat had caught and flared. For there was a savoury smell of meat in the air, together with a noise of shouting and laughter.

A servant, leaning against the pillared porch, muttered and hoped he'd be remembered before all the food was gone. He stared across the courtyards towards the pinewoods, idly counting the shadows.

Suddenly, he stood upright. There was someone coming.

The light from the palace flared again. The servant's eyes narrowed. It was a stranger—a traveller by the look of him. He was walking impudently across the courtyard.

'Be off with you!'

But the stranger did not seem to hear. He came on at a steady pace.

Within the porch, chained to the pillars, were a pair of lean, grey dogs. Their savage, bloodshot eyes were turned towards the angry servant. It was for just such an occasion as this that they were kept—their natural ferocity increased by hunger and confinement.

Eagerly the servant undid their chains. For a moment, the dogs seemed uncertain; then they snarled and padded towards the traveller. 'Kill him! Kill—!'

The servant stopped. The dogs had turned back. They were coming now towards *him*; and behind them, tall and relentless, came the traveller. His eyes were blazing.

A sudden wind swept into the palace. It burst open doors so that guards and servants hastened to close them and slide the heavy bolts. It whipped the dust from the deep-wrought cornices and sent it whirling among the columns that stood like a grove of stony trees before the banqueting hall of King Lycaon. Then that great door burst open and the leaping lights and uproar of the feasting king, his sons and their laughing wives met the traveller's eyes.

Astonished, they turned to face the interruption. The traveller stared. What had become of the creatures of Prometheus? Their faces were netted with webs of skin and their eyes gleamed without fire. It was as if the divine heat within them had proved too fierce for the Promethean clay—and cracked it. Or was it that Time, the courteous servant of the gods, had become man's arrogant overseer and marked him about the neck, eyes and brow with a hurrying whip?

'Who are you and what do you want?'

Lycaon leaned back in his gold and ivory chair. He frowned menacingly at the stranger in the doorway. Though the fellow was tall and carried himself well, his attire was humble—an insult at Lycaon's feast. His beard was golden and, in the dancing firelight, speckles of the same bright colour flickered in his deep, shadowed eyes.

'I am a traveller, Lycaon. I come from . . . the north. I ask hospitality in the name of Zeus, patron of all such as I.'

Lycaon stared at him in astonishment. 'In the name of what?'

'Zeus,' said the stranger softly. 'Do you not honour him here?'

Lycaon's astonishment seemed to increase. He stared down the table at his sons and the guests among them who had come from the farthest parts of the land to do him homage. Then he said in a tone of wonderment, 'In the name of Zeus, eh? Well, well . . . we mustn't disappoint him, must we? Holy Zeus would be angry. Hm! We might have a bad thunderstorm—' He stopped. He could contain himself no longer. He grinned; he laughed; he roared with laughter and the table joined him till the banqueting hall shook with it. Several times he pointed to the silent traveller and tried to speak; but each time laughter overcame him. At last he managed: 'You—you insolent wretch! Better—far better if you'd asked in the name of Lycaon! *He* is the only Zeus you're likely to see! Do you really imagine the kings and great ones of this world pay any heed to snivelling tales of gods? Do—do you take us for children?'

He wiped his eyes; and, with a scrape of his chair on the bronze-leafed floor, he stood up. There was a knife held loosely in his deep-veined hand. He pricked a piece of meat from the steaming bowl before him and slowly ate it.

'I am going to kill you, fellow,' he said gently—then turned to the avenue of curving lips and hooded eyes that watched eagerly. 'Shall I cut his throat, or—?'

He smiled. A woman, halfway down the table, her mouth still greasy from the feast, gazed at him with shining eyes.

'Do it, Lycaon!' she shrieked in wild excitement. 'Do it now!'

Her passion spread. Like fire it leaped from heart to heart till all the table was ablaze with it—and the king burned hottest of all.

Two of his sons ran to shut the door, to cut off the stranger's escape. It clanged to with a dreadful brazen roar . . . and the trapped stranger was seen to shudder at it.

Then all at the table rose with a squeaking clamour of sandalled feet and began to advance, pointing and laughing. The women, no less deadly than the men, jeered shrilly at the doomed, staring traveller who had dared to suppose that there was any other Olympus than the palace of Lycaon—or any other gods than the great mortals he now beheld.

'Zeus! Zeus!' shouted Lycaon, his fierce voice crowning the uproar. 'I am Zeus! See—!'

The greasy-mouthed woman was helpless with laughter. The god-like Arcadian was whistling and quacking and flapping his long, powerful arms. 'A bird! I'm a bird! A quail! A cuckoo! Beware! Zeus comes—!'

He rushed on her, screeching and beating the air. He bore down on her and she shrieked with comic alarm—

'Zeus loves! Quack-quack! Zeus nests! The god has wings!'

Silently the traveller watched. The expression on his face was strange. Those who saw it were momentarily chilled. They took it for the look of a man who has seen his own death racing down upon him. They had not seen anything like it before.

Then the woman with the king screamed eagerly: 'The feast! Give him the divine portion! Great Lycaon—make him gnaw the bones like a dog! Then the knife. Make him beg; make him bark and plead! Immortal Lycaon—!' She struggled away from the inspired king and stumbled to the table where the bowls still steamed.

Lycaon followed, panting with laughter. He dug his knife

into the great bronze jar from which all had been served. 'Here!' he shouted, to the unlucky traveller from the north. 'Lycaon gives you the gods' portion to fill your guts before you die! Beg and take it like a dog!'

Lycaon withdrew the knife and offered it, dripping with rich liquid. Hanging from its point was the bony remnant of a young man's hand. Such was the feast of Lycaon.

'Take it!' He thrust it to the full stretch of his arm; and behind him, the crowding revellers grinned as the stranger seemed to tremble and recoil.

'Lycaon commands—' began the terrible Arcadian; then he stopped. He faltered. The knife bearing the still-knotted bones seemed intolerably heavy. He looked up—and saw the stranger's eyes. They were blazing like suns in a merciless sky. Their radiance was blinding—unendurable. Lycaon could not look away. He tried to cry out; but no words came—only a queer snarling grunt of dismay. He tried to move; but a fiery pain stabbed his back.

He could not stay upright. The pain was enormous. The stranger raised his hand; and Lycaon sank under the burden of his agony. The knife clattered on the bronze floor—and the bony hand fell away and lay, seeming to beckon to his own. . . .

He reached for it. Again he gave vent to the queer snarling sound. What was happening to him? His hand! Before his eyes it was changing. The dark hairs thickened and turned grey. They covered his skin, and his fingers withered away into claws. His palms hardened and turned black.

'Bark, Lycaon,' he heard the mighty stranger say. 'Howl and whine and moan—not like a dog, but like the wolf you are!'

Then Lycaon turned and faced his sons and their wives and the guests who had come to do him homage. He glared at them with maddened, bloodshot eyes. His jaws dripped and he laid back his pointed ears. He howled for pity—and they screamed with terror. He whined and moaned for them to help him. But they turned to fly. They scrambled backwards, falling over the upturned chairs, scalding themselves in the spilled stew . . . clawing at each other desperately—shrieking in the extremity of their terror. But it was not terror of Lycaon the wolf. It was terror of the tall stranger. For the smallest instant they had seen a radiance that blistered their eyes and printed on their fading minds the image of a figure, part man-like, that shimmered in the midst of the light. Then this radiance diminished till all that remained of it was in the stranger's eyes. 'No—no—!' pleaded the sons of Lycaon. It was too late. The stranger raised his hand. . . .

Wolves ran howling and moaning through the fair palace of Lycaon. Like gaunt shadows, they flickered down passages and across halls where once they'd walked in the semblance of men and women. Their eyes were red and mad with fear—for everywhere they turned they saw the blinding vision that lingered in their brains.

Then they ran out into the moonlit courtyard and fled like grey ghosts to hide in the grim dark pinewoods of Lycaeus, to moan and howl forever under the silver arrows of the moon.

The palace of Lycaon lay quiet and still. Then a strange wind began to blow. It whistled down the empty passages and high across the empty nalls. It blew out the fires and burst open the bolted doors. Then it passed through the pillared portico, and the traveller crossed the silver courtyard, leaving Lycaon's. marble palace as still and lonely as death. The god returned to Olympus. His brow was dark with a huge anger. . . .

The wind began to blow from the south. Day and night it blew—and no other winds interrupted it. It was as if they had been imprisoned in the cave of Aeolus by divine command. Men stared up to where the south wind gathered his dark harvest. Clouds—clouds bulking in ramparts and layers of dreadful black. From all the corners of the sky the unceasing south wind piled them up like sinister towns and evil palaces of toppling weight.

In vain the wild wolves of Lycaeus howled and moaned their warnings. But none could understand them—and men fled before their savage aspect.

By night, strange unearthly mists seemed to rise from the beds of rivers and drift down towards the sea. Sometimes in these mists there seemed to be vague, naked shapes of grim and often frightening appearance.

Men who were passing saw them, and reported of it; but none could tell what they were or suspect what they were about. The conflicting passions that man had inherited prevented the blazing clarity of vision that might have told them where they were going and for what purpose. Thus what might have been done was neglected for ideas that seemed better at the time.

But far in the north, in the bitter freezing region of the Caucasus, there was one whose vision was mercilessly clear. Prometheus, the Titan, saw the hostile sky; he saw, too, the river gods go down menacingly to the council of Poseidon.

He raged in his chains as he understood what was to come. The mountains about him trembled and the wide glaciers cracked. Then he raised his vast, tragic head and shouted across the world. He shouted to his children even as the eternal vulture plucked and ate at him.

But the implacable south wind still blew, and his words whirled back and were lost.

He shouted again—across the black, starless night. Thinly, his words beat against the wind like birds whose southward journey will end in an ocean death. But this time, he was heard. In Phthia, northward of Arcadia, Deucalion started up in his bed. The words that had reached him, out of the night, seemed like a dream. Quickly he roused Pyrrha, his wife, and told her of them. She was a daughter of Pandora and Epimetheus, and had inherited much of her great father's gentleness as well as her mother's beauty. She loved and honoured Deucalion, who was a good and upright man.

'What must we do, my lord?'

'We must make a vessel sea-worthy, Pyrrha. We must do it now. So my dream has told me. We must stock the vessel with meat and grain . . . and we must pray to Zeus.'

The south wind had stopped. The air grew still and heavy. Frightened birds flew into the tree tops—and the wolves of Lycaeus whimpered at the dreadful sky.

And then it fell: the Deluge. It seemed as if a thunderbolt had been hurled at the black cities in the sky. They blazed and split and, with a mighty roar, they toppled down. Rain, such as no man had seen, rushed down in blinding torrents. It smashed the orchards and the harvests. It ran hissing down the marble columns like a plague of silver snakes to swirl round the pedestals in ever-rising coils . . . and it filled up the cradles that had been left in porches and gardens so that infants were drowned before their shrieking, gasping mothers could drag them in.

Then men who lived by the sea saw the waves writhing under the steaming torrents; and, for an instant, seemed to see a wild radiance rise out of the waters and strike them with a triple lightning. The waves reared up like ranges of black mountains and moved towards the shore. Slowly at first, then faster they came, gathering height till they were capped with foam that seemed to boil.

But they did not break and fall when they reached their natural limits. Instead they rushed on, over the sands and beaches, engulfing the stone quays of harbours, and tearing off the stout iron rings to which ships had been tied and flinging them up like black motes in the savage sky. Then the terrible waves met the advancing streams and rivers in mid-career. Up they leaped and, with double mouths, gaped at the heavens, before they fell with a wild roar and swallowed up the land.

The river gods had kept their appointment with their mighty overlord of the sea. And over and above them all, the father of the gods continued to hurl down the wrath of the sky. Almighty Zeus had resolved to wash the earth clean of the foul stain of mankind.

The gods looked down and shuddered; but they dared not oppose great Zeus who crouched like a god of stone amid his terrible clouds.

Higher and higher rose the waters, now rushing darkly through the high casements of buildings and sending up vast silver bubbles like the ghosts of murdered towns.

And everywhere, like feebly twitching flies, tossed the remnants of mankind. Some had been washed from rooftops; some had been harvested, like ripe fruit, from the topmost branches of trees. But many, many more were dead beneath the waters where they had been drowned in the treacherous safety of their homes. Eerily they moved among dim halls and passages, while strange sea-creatures nosed and nibbled them from pillar to post.

Now the waters began to creep up the slopes of the mountains where the last men had fled for refuge. At first, they helped each other, brother pulling brother up the sharp rocks and carrying wives and children in straining arms. Some even went back for those who were trapped in muddy crevices and dragged them free.

Then savage Ares, god of hateful war, opened their eyes to the dwindling land on which they were crowding together. They began to struggle and fight for their places. They began to hack at one another with such weapons as they had, and the water round the mountain tops swirled with red.

Those who still climbed were kicked back to their deaths; and one by one, those who had achieved safety were hurled from it by those who were stronger.

Fathers abandoned their children and husbands thrust out their wives. Then at last the waters put an end to their savagery and engulfed them all, dragging away the last two men who were locked in a murderous embrace. But they were not drowned. Their hands still grasped their knives which were lodged each in the belly of his brother.

At last, the black clouds drained away and the sun stared down. There was a great silence everywhere; the kingdom of Poseidon stretched over the earth like a silver winding sheet. Beneath it, the drowned palaces and proud colonnades that had once rivalled Olympus, lay like pale, uneasy dreams; and the shadowy pinewoods of Lycaeus swayed in the currents, putting out tangled branches to catch the inquiring fish—like the fingers of a nightmare.

Gigantic crabs tottered among deep forsaken market-places, and weird grey serpentine creatures wove greasy webs among the dim pillars of cold temples.

Then, in that enormous quiet, a single, tiny voice was heard. So frail and distant was it that the very words seemed unthreaded when they reached the sky and drifted like seedlings. . . .

It was a prayer. Someone was thanking the father of the gods for sparing them. The ark of Pyrrha and Deucalion had

survived the flood.

The greatest of the gods looked down and saw the small roofed vessel drifting over the shoulder of a mountain. It was Parnassus, whose twin peaks pricked up like the ears of some ancient beast turned to stone.

'Shall I strike again, brother?' great Poseidon shouted from his enlarged estate.

'Enough, brother. Return within your boundaries. Retreat, Poseidon. Go back.'

The earth-shaker scowled. The power he had tasted was sweet. But even he stood in awe of the thunderbolt.

Then greedy Hades called from his grim kingdom. 'The last two. Send them to me, brother. They are mine—'

'Peace, brother. They prayed to me. They are mine.'

'By what right?'

'By the right of my will, brother. And the thunderbolt.'

Secure in their ark, Deucalion and Pyrrha waited. The dispute between the three great brothers they heard as the muttering of distant thunder, which continued for nine nights and days. Such was the measurement of man beside the scope of the gods.

Then, suddenly, wonderfully, they felt their vessel scrape against rock. Pyrrha's lovely eyes shone. She reached for Deucalion's hands and grasped them with her own. The vessel jarred and shuddered; its endless course was halted.

'Almighty Zeus has heard our prayer. We have reached land!'

12 ● Mothers' Bones . . . Stones . . .

The waters began to drain away. At first, they moved slowly, with seeming reluctance, then with a growing haste so that everywhere there was heard a soft rushing and kissing sound as if of some gigantic farewell. Trees rose up and lifted their shining trunks aloft with sudden cascades of silver foliage. Tumbled rocks and the upper slopes of hillsides grew like dreams, with deep sighs and suckings as the water found veins and crevices in the earth to rush through. And everywhere there pricked up the million tiny spears of grass—as if multitudes of little warriors were waiting under the shrinking tide. Then the water whispered away, leaving sparkling chains and jewels to wind among the green.

At last the ocean returned to its natural boundaries, where the waves sighed and muttered as they licked at the shore. The taste of the mountains had been sweet.

The great golden sun shone down on the quiet world. Homes, palaces and temples dripped emptily. Torn robes and broken sandals littered the rooftops in attitudes of silent madness and haste. Of those who had worn them, there was no sign. It seemed as if they were all hiding—playing some enormous game—and, at any moment, would come shouting and laughing out of the silent shadows and leaping through the curtained seaweed that overhung their doors and casements. But nothing stirred, and the game grew cold.

Then, suddenly, a child's sandal, all on its own, scraped weirdly across a courtyard. It tottered back and forth as if seeking its pair. A crab had taken it for its fortress and, thus armoured, was looking for the sea.

Half way down the steeps of Mount Parnassus, Deucalion and Pyrrha looked back to where their ark lay cradled against the sky.

They were alone in the world, and frightened. Again they prayed to the father of the gods—but there was no sound save for the dripping of water as it drained from branches and dropped to the puddled ground. Tresses of green and brown weeds hung from the trees like grief-torn hair; and the groves and glades reeked of the ancient sea.

'Look!' whispered Pyrrha, her fingers tightening on her husband's hand. They had not let go of each other since they'd left their vessel. Each dreaded that if that desperate grip were broken, even for a moment, the other would be swallowed up in the universal mystery. 'Look, Deucalion!'

Pyrrha pointed as if in confirmation of a dream. High in the branches of the trees, there glinted and shone the strangest fruit.

They saw them everywhere. Little fishes that had been caught and had perished, amazed, in such unlikely nets.

More than anything, it was this weird, unnatural sight that made Deucalion and his wife feel how enormous was their loneliness.

Neither of them wept nor even whispered now. Tears and words alike had lost their meaning in the face of emptiness.

Silently they walked through the quiet glades, while everywhere the sea water dripped.

Suddenly they stopped. Their faces grew pale; their limbs trembled and their entwined fingers whitened with the fierceness of their grip.

They stood at the edge of a glade that had an air of glimmering secrecy. Within it stood a great stone basin, over which, quiet and intent, crouched a strange, uncanny youth. His bright limbs were naked, and on his feet were curious golden sandals that had wings.

He was casting stones into the basin, and watching them as they fell. He neither spoke nor turned his head. The fall and pattern of the pebbles absorbed him entirely.

Pyrrha and Deucalion knelt. They had come upon a god.

'You must go down the mountain to the temple by the river,' murmured Hermes, reading from the Muses' five stones. 'And there you must pray. Your prayers will be answered, I promise you. But think carefully on the answer you receive. Consider it well before you act.'

The god gave a sideways smile. 'It is all in the stones, my friends. Believe me. . . .'

The temple was dark and cold. Water lay in smooth black pools on the stony floor and dimly reflected the roof. Thick ropes of weed clung round the ankles of the pillars and draped the forsaken altar like the careless garments of some nymph gone bathing in her stream.

'The god in the glade bade us pray,' whispered Deucalion as he and Pyrrha knelt before the altar. 'He promised we would be heard. He promised it was all in the stones. . . .'

His words drifted aloft and set up echoes amid the tall columns: stones—stones—stones—till they sank into a silence. This silence seemed to grow deeper and more absolute as Pyrrha and Deucalion knelt, gazing humbly into the black, still water that lay about the altar's foot.

For long minutes they knelt thus; and no answer came. Then, very, very softly, the echoes seemed to return. A hundred tiny voices seemed to be murmuring, their words all overlapping till the air in the temple was set beating and quivering. 'Stones . . . stones . . . bones . . . bones . . . mother's bones . . . mother's —mother's—cast them—throw them—mother's bones—' The dark water shook and trembled. Strange flickering lights appeared in it, like the reflection of countless fireflies. 'Mothers' bones—cast them—shoulders—shoulders—walk—bones of mothers—mothers—'

Then all the voices died away and a single utterance of vast gentleness whispered: 'Take the bones of your mother and cast them over your shoulders as you walk away.'

The silence flooded back. Deucalion and Pyrrha left the dark temple for the shining solitude of the world outside.

'The bones of our mother?' murmured Pyrrha; she shivered.

Deucalion stared about him. The quiet mountain was littered with stones and pebbles the sea had wrenched from river-beds.

'It is all in the stones.' Wonderingly, Deucalion repeated the god's words. Then his eyes widened. 'The stones! Pyrrha— are they not the bones of earth, the mother of us all? Pyrrha— it is in the stones! We must gather them and walk down the mountain, casting them behind us. The stones. Pyrrha! Quick —gather as many as you can carry!'

Chiefly the stones were smooth and greyish-white, but here and there were shining, deeply coloured pebbles of green, blue and brown with delicate veinings. They had come from remoter parts and had been left by the careless sea.

It was Pyrrha who gathered these—while Deucalion, in his greater haste, contented himself with the more plentiful grey.

At last, when they could carry no more, they began to walk down the mountain, sometimes stumbling under the weight of the stones they had cradled in their gowns. And one by one— as the voice in the temple had commanded—they cast the stones over their shoulders and heard them fall on grass or rock.

They did not look back.

It was Deucalion who cast the last stone; and when this was done, he reached out once more for his wife's hand. Together they stumbled towards the silent valley, still not daring to look back. Then they halted, holding fast to each other. No sound came from behind them. All they heard was their own beating hearts and panting breath.

Yet they knew the prickling sense of being watched. They turned, and stared back at the mountain.

Pyrrha cried out, and tears of joyful wonderment stood in Deucalion's eyes.

The mountain was stirring; it seemed to be glimmering with movement. The sun shone down, catching the quick gleamings amid the trees and between the rocks.

Shy faces peered down; briefly vanished, then peeped again, inquisitively. Hands, arms, shoulders bloomed in the long grass . . . and where the last stone had fallen, a young man crouched with his chin in his hands, gazing at Pyrrha and Deucalion with grave curiosity. His eyes were grey, like the stone; but they shone with a mortal eagerness.

He stood up and, with a wide gesture, encompassed all the valleys and hills and richly wooded countryside that the mountain overlooked.

'All this,' he said wonderingly, 'belongs to us?'

13 ● The Lady of the Harvests

Of all the Olympian gods and goddesses, it was Demeter who loved the earth best. The very skirts of her gown had been drenched in the sweeping flood; for she'd lingered in her fields, unable to take her farewell.

And while the waters had covered the world, she'd wandered desolately across the barren sky whose stars and milky clouds pleased her less than daisies in the grass.

Then, when the waters sank, the great goddess smiled again and in her heart declared herself for man. She blessed the harvests, and her gentle spirit was ever in the fields and granaries; and in the long evenings, she loved to take her ease in some countryman's home and listen to the talk of sunshine and grain, and new shoots and old trees and the mischief-making nymphs.

None of mankind remembered the flood—for its memory only burned in the brains of wolves, creatures accursed by gods and men.

Though the goddess never came in her blinding Olympian glory, there were few who did not know her for an immortal; and in many a home, an honoured place was kept at table, never to be sat in till the great gleaming lady came again.

Indeed, she was more of a stranger to Olympus; and in the high council-chamber her gold and ivory throne stood empty far more often than did those rush-and-pinewood chairs kept for her by the brief tenants of her pastures and fields.

Her sister Hera, the proud queen of Heaven, condemned her for this—and declared contemptuously that the hot lady Demeter was over-fond of tumbling in the hay with her stone-eyed muddy mortals.

But almighty Zeus frowned warningly and bade great Hera

hold her tongue. Though the lord of the sky did not choose to admit it, he had himself tumbled in the hay with fair Demeter; and the child she'd borne was of Olympian stock. It had been a daughter and her name was Persephone . . . though Zeus and Demeter, between themselves, still called her Core, on account of a comical sound she'd made when first she'd begun to talk. 'Core . . . Core . . .' it had sounded like; and even the two immortals had been unable to make more sense of it than that.

She inherited much of her mother's gentleness, together with a passion for flowers. Poppies were her favourites, and she loved to gather them among the fields of Enna, in Sicily, with her little court of nymphs.

Sometimes when Demeter would come in search of her, the goddess would see nothing but the nodding cornfield speckled with scarlet blossoms. She'd call: 'Persephone—Persephone! Core, my child!' But there'd be no answer.

Then perhaps a crow would fly up . . . and all at once the myriad flowers would seem to explode into the air in a scarlet storm. With shrieks and fearsome cries, Persephone and her wild nymphs would rise up and pelt the laughing goddess with poppy-heads till she sank, helpless with laughter, amid the bending spears of corn. Then she'd open wide her golden arms and Persephone, still fierce with flowers, would fly into that citadel—and be armisticed with kisses.

Sometimes, it was true, even as proud Hera had declared, the great lady of the harvests would honour some particular mortal with her embraces. But she was not alone in this. Other goddesses and gods had been snared by the haunting charms of the frail creatures of Prometheus. For, though Zeus had created them anew, they were still the children of the tragic Titan's vast brain. Their tenancy of the earth was still brief; and to the immortals it seemed no more than an afternoon. Perhaps it was this that drew the Olympians down into arms whose loveliness had to be caught on the wing of time before it withered away.

Golden Demeter, walking the world, would many a time feel the prick at her heart when she came into some well-remembered room and found more chairs than her own standing empty.

'So soon?' she'd murmur. 'Have they gone to my grim brother's kingdom so soon?'

'They were old,' would come the sad reply: and the goddess would shake her lovely head. Then perhaps some infant would be brought to her for blessing, and she would smile and marvel that hope could be renewed.

But Persephone was always young and lovely, and swept dark dreams away. So Demeter would go to Sicily again, and call across the fields of Enna till the poppies blazed and whirled.

'Core! Core!' The goddess called to her child. The sun stood high and the crumpled poppies trembled faintly in the nodding sea of gold. Then they grew still again. . . .

'Core! Core!' The goddess clapped her hands. At once a cloud of crows flew up, tattering the bright air with their black wings.

'Core—Core!' they screeched, as if in harsh mockery. This time, the field was empty, and Demeter frowned. A shadow crossed her heart as the memory of empty chairs crept over the empty cornfield like a ghost.

No . . . no. Demeter shook her immortal head. Her Core was not subject to the three blind sisters and their dreadful shears; nor was her joy and brightness destined to be quenched in grim Hades' cold, lightless halls.

The goddess smiled and gathered up her gown that was embroidered with yellow and violet flowers. She had remembered that Persephone loved the meadows of Arcadia almost as much as Sicilian Enna. Most certainly she was in Arcadia. . . .

But even as Demeter's chariot rose and the clustering golden spears bent and swayed under the wind of her going, the goddess started. Peering from a wood that fringed the deserted cornfield, the goddess fancied she saw one of her daughter's attendant nymphs. She fancied that the nymph's eyes had been wild and dismayed; and that she had been watching the goddess with terror.

Then the scene whirled away as the chariot sped . . . and great Demeter brushed it from her mind.

But Persephone was not in Arcadia, nor was she in neighbouring Attica.

'Core—Core!' cried Demeter. The rich, wide cornfields stirred only with the breeze; and the dappling poppies lay as still as drops of blood.

So she rode to Crete; and for the first time there was fear in a goddess's heart.

'Core—Core!' she called across the island's rippled meadows and down the hillside pastures. She waited—then, as before in Sicily, a cloud of crows rose screaming out of the gold, their ragged wings flickering in a pattern of fatal black. Demeter fled.

Now began her great search. From land to land she rushed, crying and calling across fields and riverbanks and wherever the gay flowers grew. When night came, she left her chariot and, with two flaming torches of pine held aloft, stumbled through meadows that had been empty by day—as if she thought the sun had cheated her. Fearfully, men and women looked out from their mansions and cottages and saw the moving blaze twisting and jerking among the dark pastures, then darting into some nearby wood where the trees suddenly leaped out in attitudes of black dismay. Sometimes shepherds, sleeping out in the gentle night, would waken and see her coming. Her lovely face in the torchlight would be all rippled with shadows and scarlet light; and her golden eyes would be wild. Then they'd bury their frightened faces in the grass; and in the morning think it a dream—till they saw the trail of grey, feathery wood ash, that lay like a streamer of bereavement and marked the goddess's passing.

'Core—Core!' Men in the fields stopped and grew pale when the goddess's voice was heard. 'Core—Core!'

The sound, once sweet, now sighed and moaned across the world like the wailing of some bleak and bitter wind. It echoed through the pillared halls of palaces, and under the sleeping eaves of cottages so that children would waken and cry out wildly—as if they would answer the mighty mother who searched and called for her lost child.

The corn withered and shrivelled in the husk; the gold turned brown and the harvested fields resembled weird grave-yards where the stiff and scanty sheaves leaned like broken memorials to the riches of yesterday. Demeter's blessings had been used up; the ever-searching goddess's heart was emptied of all but an aching fear.

'Core—Core!'

Birds flew up in speckled throngs and sped southward to escape Demeter's terrible cries . . . and in the woods and forests, small creatures fought over the last of the nuts and

berries from the dying trees. Some hid pitiful stores in secret hollows, to prolong their lives for scanty months; others thinly stretched themselves on the bare ground, whimpered and perished, even as the grieving goddess passed.

'Core—Core!'

Desolately the goddess wandered till she came at last to the harsh stony mountain in whose deep cleft the three blind sisters crouched.

Clotho's wheel creaked and whistled as the bright thread grew . . . to be measured and cut, measured and cut by the hateful shears.

The sound they made was neat and quick and as they pounced on the stretched thread, they flashed like the wings of a bitter silver crow.

'A goddess is near us,' mumbled Clotho, rocking back and forth at her wheel. 'I feel her light.'

'There's a smell of corn and poppies in the air,' croaked sinewy Lachesis. 'It is great Demeter.'

But shrunken Atropos, her coarse white robes stained with sweat, only nodded. She kept her breath to wield the terrible shears. Nothing stopped her; nothing slowed her, and the mighty goddess gazed in dread as the cut threads fell like rain.

They lay on the stony ground in a mad profusion and the goddess began to pull and pluck at them. Her great search had led her to this, the last place in the universe.

But she found no severed strand that was bright enough to have been her daughter's life.

'Why so short, why so quick?' she whispered as she stared once more at the toiling Three.

'You should know, great Demeter,' grinned Clotho, turning her ancient blind face this way and that till she felt the full force of the goddess's light.

'Without your blessing the yarn comes thin,' muttered Lachesis. 'It must be cut short.'

Then Clotho raised an arm that seemed no more than naked bone, bandaged with yellowed skin. She pointed to the gnarled thorn bush. 'Soon there will be nothing left for us to do. The wool grows scarce. The huge goats no longer climb this way. Their strength is failing; their pastures have shrivelled and died.'

'No!' cried the goddess in a sudden anguish. 'Stop!' She seized the dreadful Atropos by the wrist so that the shears fell open and a frail strand lay waiting between the blades.

'Begone, great goddess!' snarled Atropos, and shook herself free. 'We are not subject to you.'

The shears snapped shut. The thread divided and fell. And Demeter fancied that she heard across the world a faint cry, then a sigh, and a ripple of tears. . . .

'Core—Core!' wept mighty Demeter. 'My heart is emptied of everything save you! It is cold, my child; cold and dark as the Kingdom of the Dead. Core—Core!'

Then the goddess's voice faded and dwindled away till it was no more than the sighing of the wind that mingled with the creaking of Clotho's wheel and the ceaseless snapping of shears.

14● 'Core . . . Core . . .'

Close by Eleusis, in Attica, there was a home that had seen better days. Some said that it had once been a palace. Certainly, parts were very old and were pillared with a crumbling grandeur quite out of keeping with the newer part that had been built in the ancient forecourt.

This cottage—for so it was—squatted with unkempt thatch, like some ragged child in the shadow of its ruined father, as if listening to tales of long ago: to tales of when the crops grew and the harvests were golden, and when the wind was not so bitter nor the nights so cold.

This dreaming on former glories was shared by the family who lived there; but otherwise they were hospitable and kindly enough. Provided travellers would sit and listen to their harmless boasts, they would entertain them to the very best of their slender substance. Kings could have done no more. Only a boy called Abas, one of their sons, ever disgraced them with any show of insolence. For this boy lived too much in the pillared ruins where he strutted and postured with as dry and scaly an arrogance as the long-dead past.

To him, all strangers were beggars and targets for his childish contempt.

Thus, when the tall woman came, knocking on the door and asking for something to drink, Abas pushed past his grandmother and stood menacingly in the doorway as if the thirsty woman was some vagrant thief.

Her gown, embroidered with yellow and violet flowers, had once been beautiful; but now it was much torn and muddied about the hem—as if she had been wandering among gorse and thorns in search of something.

This air of searching was very strong. Even as she waited

patiently for the drink that was being fetched, her eyes kept turning this way and that so restlessly that the contemptuous Abas could scarce make out whether they were brown, blue or as golden as her wind-wild hair.

'What are you looking for, beggar woman?' he asked. 'Something to steal?'

Momentarily the woman's eyes flashed. Then she frowned and shook her head, and tried to smile as if she well knew the ways of children.

'No,' she answered softly. 'I am looking for—for my child.'

'There's been no beggar brats round here,' said Abas coldly. 'So you'd best be on your way.'

Just then, the boy's grandmother returned with a pitcher of barley water into which she'd sprinkled some refreshing mint. Abas frowned as the old woman poured it into a finely carved stone cup. This was singularly ancient and was considered one of the chief treasures of their home. Not even he was allowed to drink from it; and now it was offered to the vagrant woman whose stained gown fluttered out its rents and tears like the very banners of poverty.

Suddenly a baby cried and a woman's voice called from within. The grandmother excused herself and left the stranger to drink her fill.

But Abas stayed.

'If I ruled this house,' he said, 'such as you would be drinking from something very different.'

The strange woman lowered the cup. She stared at the boy. Some grains of barley had caught at the corner of her mouth.

'From the trough,' sneered Abas. 'For you drink like a pig.'

The strange woman's eyes no longer turned. They were fixed upon Abas. Uneasily, he saw they were indeed golden and dreadfully bright. They dazzled and burned. He licked his lips, which had grown as dry as dust. He couldn't help himself. His tongue kept flicking in and out.

Then this woman raised her hand. Abas stared and glared till his eyes bulged from his narrow head. She seemed to be growing taller and taller. She towered into the sky above him. Terrified, he turned to fly into the cottage. But he could not.

The once humble step rose like a mighty wall above his head. Then he tried to scream. An enormous hammer, shaped like his grandmother's foot, loomed over him and began to sweep down to crush him flat.

'Go!' he heard a whisper that yet seemed to fill the universe. 'Hide your ugly little soul among the crumbling stones! Even the pig trough is too big for you now!'

So the tiny little creature that had once been the insolent Abas scuttled away, his lips still dry as dust from the heat of great Demeter's anger. Gentle though her nature was, in that unlucky moment she had become again the daughter of savage Cronus and the sister of unpitying Zeus.

'Have you drunk your fill, my dear?'

The grandmother smiled and asked the strange tall woman if she needed anything more.

Then something moved rapidly from just under her foot. She looked down and shuddered with faint disgust as a little spotted lizard, its forked tongue flickering in and out, scuttled away to hide among the cracked pillars and broken stones of the old house.

'Forgive me for leaving you so,' went on the old woman as the stranger silently bowed her head, 'but my daughter has a new son—and in these times of death and famine. . . .' Her voice drifted into nothingness; then she smiled as if apologising to the stranger for mentioning so commonplace a matter as hunger and suffering. The old woman, whose wrinkled, fading eyes had already seen a lifetime's losses dwindle into memories, looked up and tried to catch the tall stranger's eye—as if to share mortality with her.

'You're welcome to dine with us, my dear. And we can offer shelter for the night. Abas!' she called abruptly. 'Abas!' She looked to the stranger. 'Did you see the boy go?'

The woman nodded and started towards the pillared ruin. Her eyes were blazing with uncanny tears.

Suddenly a chill crossed the grandmother's heart. She could not account for it; so she said no more and led the stranger inside the cottage.

The old woman's daughter lay on a couch made up by the fire. She was pale and thin, but her eyes gleamed warmly in the firelight as she cradled her infant child.

The tall stranger smiled down on her almost enviously.

'You must understand,' said the mother, raising her head, 'that we've come down in the world. As you must have seen, the house was once much grander. Indeed, my husband's family used to be quite important people . . . princes, I think. But times have changed—and what with this terrible famine, we have to live in a way we're not at all accustomed to.' The stranger nodded; her smile grew gentler.

'But we'll make you welcome, nonetheless. Though we are poor, we are still human, you know. . . .'

So the stranger sat by the fire, and while the old woman crept away to prepare a meal, her daughter chattered on of bygone times and family splendours. It seemed she had high hopes of the infant she cradled, and firmly believed he'd restore the glory of their name. Once, she'd had such hopes of her last-born son, Abas—but he lacked gentleness and respect. Her other sons, who in turn had been hoped for, were worthy, but more of farmers than anything else, and had much of the land's roughness. Even Eubuleus, who'd travelled as far as Sicily to see more of the high-born world, had returned only to write wild poetry and look after swine.

The mother frowned and sighed. 'Have you any children?' she asked abuptly.

The stranger nodded sadly. 'A daughter.'

'Grown up and married, I hope? And soon with children of her own?'

'No . . . no. She is young. She is always young.'

'Oh, I shouldn't worry. She'll grow up when the time comes. Where is she now?'

'I am searching for her—'

At this, the mother fell silent. The strange woman's words held an aching grief. She stilled her tongue till the meal was brought; and after it, watched the intricate castles in the fire. Now and again, she stole a glance at the stranger and had to admit to herself that the woman, despite her torn gown and wild hair, was more handsome than anyone she'd ever seen. She was thankful her husband was away—else surely he'd have been dazzled by her.

The grandmother also watched the stranger; but her glances were uneasy; and once, when their eyes met, the old woman grew pale. . . .

'Give me the child,' said the stranger softly. 'I will nurse him while you go and rest and sleep through the night.'

The mother was about to protest—when the old woman prevented her. It would be discourteous, she said, to refuse the stranger's offer . . . and all would benefit from it. Let the stranger nurse the child: her hands were soft and her breast was deep. See—how the little one looked at her! See, see! Already he stretched out his arms! 'Come, daughter . . . set your heart at rest. No harm will come to the little one!'

The grandmother took the baby from its mother and gave it into the stranger's large, fine hands. Then she and her still unwilling daughter retired into another room for the night.

For a long while, Demeter held the baby in her arms and the firelight seemed to translate both of them into dancing gold. She looked down upon the child's untroubled face, and her arms tightened round his warm soft limbs. 'Core . . . Core . . .' she whispered.

'What was that?' came the mother's drowsy voice.

'Nothing, my daughter,' murmured the old woman. 'Only the wind in the eaves. Sleep . . . sleep. . . .'

By the fire, the goddess waited . . . waited for the faint sounds from the bedchamber to die away into the gentle murmuring of sleep.

Then she stood up. 'Come, little one, even as I punished Abas, so I will reward you for—for the sake of all mothers. You will not die, little one. You and I will conquer the Fates. Come . . . come . . . Demeter will make you immortal.'

The mother turned and muttered in her sleep. A troubled frown kept brushing across her face like a web. She lifted her hand as if to dispel it. 'No . . . no . . .' she mumbled.

A strange dream had come into her mind. A vision, at first vague and undetermined, of three vast creatures in coarse white robes. Their faces turned this way and that, for they were blind. Then, all three turned full upon the sleeper's inward eye.

They laughed—and drew up what seemed to be a strand of wool.

Then one plucked at it—

The mother awoke with a cry. There was a sharp pain in her heart. She felt terror. Darkness and silence all round her.

What was happening by the fire? Her son—her son!

Trembling, she rose from her bed.

'Sleep—sleep!' whispered the old woman, and her voice shook as if in mortal terror.

But love and fear had deafened and blinded the mother to all but her inner ear and eye.

She pushed open the door. The fire cast a strange wild shadow on the wall. The mother caught her breath. She turned, she stared, she screamed. The terrible stranger was washing her child in the fire. He twisted and turned as the flames licked round his arms and neck, and the points of his eyelashes burned like tiny scarlet jewels. The woman's face was smiling with enormous gentleness as she held the infant by his ankle in the very heart of the murderous fire.

The mother screamed again and flung herself upon the stranger. She touched her, caught at her robe, then fell back in dismay. The woman was looking down at her.

'Do you not know me?' she murmured.

Helplessly the mother nodded, and hid her face in the hem of mighty Demeter's gown.

'I would have made your child immortal,' whispered the goddess; 'I would have burned away the last of his mortality. But the Fates sent you in to prevent it . . . Instead, I promise you he will become even greater than your family was in the old days.' Here the goddess smiled. 'He will restore your home to more than its former glories.'

'My daughter did not know. Forgive her, forgive her, great goddess!'

The grandmother was standing in the doorway, her tired old eyes blinking furiously before the radiance of Demeter.

'She has,' cried the mother, recovering from her awe, and clasping her unharmed son. 'He will be a king—or a prince, at the very least. Great Demeter promised.'

The goddess by the fire gazed at the joyful mother and her child and the old woman, who smiled so serenely at her generations. Demeter shook her head. There was laughter where there should have been tears. Though the Fates might cut them off, they could not put them out! What was immortality measured against a crown! Not the gods but Prometheus the Titan had made them; their spirit was not divine, it was Titanic. Now the goddess would be on her way to take up her endless search. The sight of the happy mother and her child opened up afresh the agony of the loss of Core. But they would not let her go. They begged and implored the goddess to stay till the men came back. They were expected directly. They had been out in the woods and fields calling in cattle that had strayed in search of vanished pasture. There would be a feast, as great as could be provided; chairs would be set, even as they were in the old days. Eubuleus would recite his poem. Here the grandmother frowned and looked doubtful, but Demeter laughed and agreed.

So once again the gleaming lady seated herself in one of the rush-and-pinewood chairs that, as always, were dearer to her than her golden throne on Olympus. And once again, when the men came back from the fields, she sat, a little apart, listening to their tales.

'Go on! Go on!' the mother kept urging the large, hairy youth who sat at the end of the table in modest shadows. 'Great Demeter would hear your poem.'

The youth blushed and bit his lip. He mumbled protestingly that it was not so much a poem as something that had happened to him. He didn't think that the great goddess wanted to hear how he had lost his pigs.

'Not the pigs,' said his mother irritably. 'The part about the black horses and the screaming girl. You remember—the part where you heard the thud and thunder of hooves when you were in the cornfield, and then when you saw those four gigantic black horses rushing down on you, and the golden chariot they were drawing, with the rider all in monstrous black. And, you remember, he had his arm about that beautiful young girl, and she was screaming and crying. And you said the whole earth seemed to split open and all this wild sight dashed down into the darkness. And—'

'—And my pigs went in too,' said Eubuleus glumly.

'No, not your pigs,' said his mother. 'I remember you said that the last thing you saw of them was the girl's hand outstretched and clutching a bunch of poppies.'

The goddess by the fire was standing. Her face was pale; her eyes were blazing.

'Where was this cornfield?'

'In Sicily. Just outside a town called Enna.'

'*Core!*' screamed the goddess. '*It was Core!*'

15● Spring in Hell

Wild of aspect and terrible in her anguish, the great goddess stood before her greater brother on the rocky steeps of high Olympus. The clouds trembled and the stars crept frightened into their holes as Demeter cursed the sky that had looked down on the rape of her child by Hades, hateful god of the dead.

'Nor will I bless the earth again, brother, till Core returns. All will die, mighty Zeus. The rich wide garden will shrivel and crack till Hades inherits it all. Apollo and Artemis will shine on slowly-turning emptiness and death. The bright nymphs and earth-spirits will fly into the void and be lost in eternity. Even Poseidon will raise his trident against you. In all the universe only grim Hades will stretch out his dark hand towards you. I swear it, brother. I swear it by the River Styx.'

The lord of the sky shuddered and his golden brow grew heavy as Demeter took the oath that none of the gods might break.

'Hades is a great god,' said Zeus at length, staring down on the bleak, leafless trees and the blind, grey earth. 'It is no little thing, sister, for our child to be his queen.'

'What has young Core to do with that grim king?' raged Demeter. 'What flowers are there in his cold fields; what sun, what air, what light? She loved music, great Zeus. Now she must hear the groans of the damned and the sighs of the forgotten. Is that to be her wedding hymn? She loved the fruits of the earth: what is there now for her wedding feast but the dust of bones?'

Hot tears ran down Demeter's cheeks and dropped scalding on the mountain rock. All her immortal beauty was grown stony with misery; even her rich breasts—between which Zeus himself had once laid his head—seemed dry and cold as marble.

'Core—Core!' she wept. 'If you are lost to me for ever, what do I care if the universe dies?'

The father of the gods stared at the tragic goddess and brooded on the calamity of her oath. His gigantic mind stretched itself till it encompassed all teeming creation, reaching into the farthest crannies where secret creatures thought themselves forgotten and unwatched. Then he weighed the tiniest cry against the loudest uproar of storms . . . for everything had its place.

He called for Hermes, his messenger.

'Go,' commanded Zeus. 'Go to my brother Hades and bid him free Persephone. It is my decree. But—' The lord of the sky frowned as the bright messenger trembled on the air. 'But if she has tasted of the food of the dead, then she must remain in darkness forever. This is the decree of the Fates.'

He turned to the goddess whose eyes were radiant. 'You have angered them, sister; and they have their powers. Go, Hermes —to the kingdom of the dead.'

The air grew briefly fiery; the clouds parted—then drifted slowly down the gleaming funnel made by the messenger's flight, till the print of his staff, his outstretched arms and the curious wings of his sandals dreamed and rolled away. . . .

Hermes took the path that Zeus and his brothers had taken long ago, when they'd freed the ancient prisoners of Tartarus. This was through the grove of black poplars that grew by the ocean. He sped high over the quiet River Styx, flickering in the thick air so that Charon, the fleshless boatman, looked up and wondered at a star so far from the sky. Then, on the farther bank, Cerberus, dread hound of hell, raised its three huge heads, swaying them hither and thither so that its fierce red eyes seemed to smear the night with blood.

The god flew on, now over the grey spotted Fields of Asphodel where the vague dead rustled like dry, invisible leaves. Beyond, like two tarnished mirrors, lay the pools of Memory and Forgetfulness, partly overhung by thin white trees which nodded as they dropped their bitter berries. . . .

Multitudinous ghosts clustered about them, moving desolately from one to the other as they sought to quench pain with pain.

The messenger shuddered at the scope of the dark kingdom whose gloomy plains stretched to eternal loneliness. He thought of bright Persephone moving across them—and he sped fast and faster yet till he came at last to the palace of Hades, grim counterpart of high Olympus.

Black and huge it stood before him, wrapped in a brooding silence.

The ranked pillars of towering jet that guarded the portico suddenly gleamed with tall streaks of silver as the god passed between them. Then they sank into their old blackness: the god was within.

Down endless corridors Hermes flickered, turning this way and that as sudden walls menaced him with his own shadow and turned his staff into a weapon of snakes.

Deeper and deeper he pierced into the labyrinth, till the darkness began to burn and glow and the carved cornices were painted with wrinkled gold.

Little by little the glow grew stronger as the god sped on towards the source of it. Little by little it turned the paved floor into a brazen river that ran between dark golden trees reaching up to a crazed and cracked golden sky from which blind carbuncles, opals and dim grey diamonds stared down like a universe of dead stars.

Such were the riches of Hades, lord of the dead.

'What do you want with me?'

Immortal Hermes had entered the presence of the god.

Vast Hades, crouching on his heavy throne, scowled down at the sleek bright messenger from distant Olympus.

'Yours is a rich kingdom, uncle,' said Hermes, glancing courteously round at the endless, brooding gold.

'Mine is a lonely kingdom,' said the god harshly.

'Indeed?' The god of thieves, drawing designs on the engraved floor with his staff, looked up. 'I understand that it is not so lonely as it used to be.'

Hades' scowl deepened. Savage fires seemed to spring up in the caverns of his eyes.

'The Lady Persephone,' went on Zeus's messenger, staring now at the crusted roof, now at the rich carvings that swelled and twisted from the walls till they seemed to drip in a slow metallic torrent. 'Great Demeter's child.'

'What do you want? Speak plain; for once.'

But Hermes was not given to plain speech. He smiled and flickered to the side of the dreadful throne, even overhanging it. . . .

'Between you and me, uncle, I understand she is not happy here. They say she grows thin and pale and spends her time in weeping. She will not eat with you . . . Though it's no affair of mine, Lord Hades, I fancy some nymph or goddess of a more yielding nature than Demeter's child would make a more agreeable queen.'

'Is that the message from my great brother?'

Immortal Hermes sighed, and put away tact. 'My father bids you free Persephone, Lord Hades.'

'No . . . no. . . .'

The god's whisper seemed to fill his terrible palace so that all its dead substance whispered with him. 'No . . . no . . .'

Then Hermes raised his herald's staff and reminded the huge, crouching Hades that he, like all creation, was subject to the thunderbolt. Hades raised his eyes. There was bleak hatred in them; and a grief as wild and savage as Demeter's.

'Persephone. . . .'

Once more the brazen labyrinth echoed with the god's whisper, till it seemed to waiting Hermes that all the kingdom of the dead was muttering, 'Persephone . . . Persephone. . . .'

Then she came. The layered air began to move as a vague warmth stole upon it. The cracked columns that stood at the chamber's entrance like an iron forest began to wink and gleam as if to a wandering sunrise in a flowered gown.

'Persephone!'

The child of Zeus and Demeter stood before the dark throne.

She swayed slightly and touched at a rent in the shoulder of her gown. Then she raised her bright, sad eyes and stared at her terrible lover while her radiance softly flooded the room. The gold began to gleam and shine and the vaulted ceiling blushed into a sky of jewels that danced in the light. The dull chamber seemed changed into a marvellous casket, most intricately wrought. It was full of nymphs and Tritons and ferns and strange stories told in the devious walls.

'Persephone!'

Hermes marvelled and understood why grim Hades had dared to challenge the power of Olympus.

She had come from the gardens that stretched beyond the palace . . . and a withered, white-haired creature had followed her in. He was a gardener and his name was Ascalaphus. Painfully he watched her, with eyes like a pair of blasted moons.

His arms, long and sinewy from reaching up to prune the black, quiet trees, now hung down, and his thin fingers were spread as if everywhere in the young goddess's wake he found the ghosts of flowers.

'Since I cannot make you happy, Persephone, you must return.' Hades' words came slow and gratingly, as if they were being forced from cracking iron.

Demeter's child looked unbelievingly at the huge dark god. Her lips parted in the amazement of her joy.

'I loved you, Persephone,' whispered Hades. 'But that was not enough.' Tears as red as blood were coursing down his shadowy cheeks.

'Go! Go!' he shouted suddenly; and his voice sent the brazen echoes rolling down the corridors till the columns trembled and the walls shook.

'You'll not regret this, uncle,' murmured Hermes hastily; and began to draw bright Persephone back from the throne and towards the pillared entrance of the chamber. 'All creation will applaud your wise and generous act.'

But the god, watching the sweet light go, groaned only, 'Persephone . . . Persephone. . . .'

Already she was among the iron trees and the eternal chamber of Hades was sinking into its gigantic, gilded gloom. The bright stars died and the stories in the walls ended in the weight of hanging nightmare.

'The gods will honour you,' came Hermes' dwindling voice, winding back among the pillars, 'and even the hard Fates will nod their heads, uncle. For this is their wish, too. Persephone must return, they decreed, if she has eaten no food of the dead.'

No food of the dead. . . . The herald's voice seemed to ripple among the columns like a tide receding.

'*No food of the dead?*'

Ascalaphus, the hideous gardener, awoke from his withered dream with a shriek. He began to choke and cough and shout

126

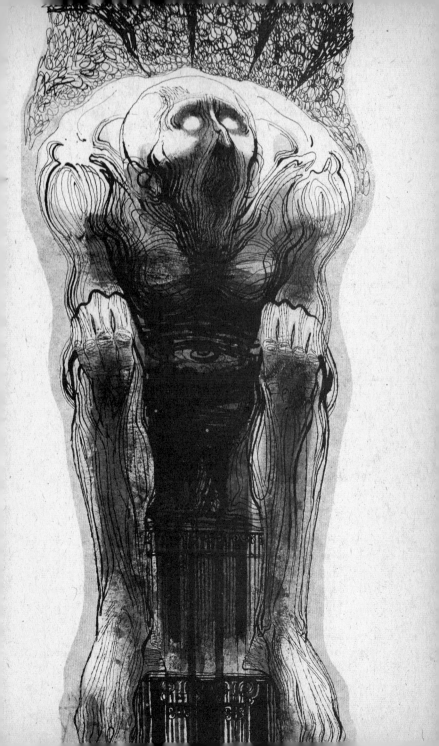

with malignant laughter.

'Seven seeds!' he screeched. 'She ate seven seeds! I saw her! Pomegranate seeds—red as her blood!'

The dreadful creature was capering up and down in triumph and waving his arms like shabby wings. 'Now she must stay! Now she must walk *my* gardens and gather *my* flowers for ever!'

They met at Eleusis; the goddess and her lost child. And though the frantic joy of their meeting seemed to make a little summer in the midst of the stricken land, it was only at Eleusis. Such joy as this could neither spread nor endure. Its substance was tears; its purpose—farewell. Persephone was for the kingdom of Hades; Demeter was for the eternal winter of the world.

'The Fates! The Fates!' screeched the hellish gardener, whose tongue had damned Demeter and her child. He clung to the rim of the great goddess's chariot-wheel as if to prevent its escape. Dead, bent and dusty, he blinked enviously in the light of day.

'I was the instrument of the Fates!'

'Then be forever hated,' cursed wild Demeter, 'like the malignant hags themselves!'

She raised her hand and struck him across the mouth. At once, that venomous thing split and gaped. The skin shrivelled, and hardened into beaked bone. Then the face about it shrank and darkened till the bright, spiteful eyes all but engulfed it. His long arms, beating and flailing against horrible pain, bent and cracked and splintered into changed shapes—and the flesh was torn into feathers. He shrieked and screamed—but no longer in words.

'Foul creature, begone!'

At the goddess's command, it rose, still screaming, from her chariot-wheel and beat raggedly away to hide itself forever in those gnawed-off scraps of hell that still littered the world of day. A screech-owl ever doomed to hoot disaster in the midst of joy!

Demeter forsook the company of gods and men. She wept no more, as if she feared her very tears might nourish the world she'd cursed. Haggard and terrible, she broke through the naked forests where the beasts died and the streams froze. Sometimes she would kneel and gaze down into the thick ice to where the caught nymph or genius of the waters lay staring up, pierced with needles of broken crystal. Anguish answered anguish, and the goddess moved on.

One by one her sisters and brothers in immortality pleaded with her, but to each and all of them she had given the same reply:

'Core—Core! Give me back my child!'

At last she trailed her desolate gown back into Attica. She wandered across the barren lap of Mount Hymettus where the wild bees used to make honey for the gods. The once fair garden of ancient Prometheus crumbled under her feet. Suddenly, she stumbled and cried out in pain. A potsherd had cut her heel. She bent to pick it up. Was it from the very jar in which the Titan had kept the substance he had fashioned into man? Demeter shook her head. What did it matter now? All labour was in vain. . . .

'Demeter, my child.'

The goddess looked up. Though sinking into ruin, parts of the Titan's house still stood. The voice that called her had come from within.

'Demeter—great goddess of the harvests!'

Slowly, she entered the house. It was cold and rank. Rooms had fallen one into another, and all that remained of the strange chamber where Prometheus had laboured was the withered fig-tree.

'Demeter.' A mighty figure was crouching beside its trunk. It was Rhea, mother of Creation and of Demeter herself.

'Great goddess—you must relent!'

'Give me back my child!'

'I, too, lost children—even you, Demeter.'

'But they returned.'

'Only to be lost again.' Rhea's unfathomed eyes stared at her daughter whose grief was destroying the world. 'Listen,' she whispered. She held up her hand, and Demeter heard from high amid the ragged mountains of the north the screaming of Prometheus in his chains.

'The vulture still flies,' muttered Demeter.

'Not the vulture,' said Rhea, 'but you, my daughter. Prometheus weeps for the world.'

Demeter bowed her head, and sank at her mother's feet.

'Give me back my child.'

Rhea's hand lost itself in the rich gold of her daughter's hair.

'Yes . . . yes. . . . She will return, and return again. There will be meetings, Demeter. There will be great broad days of joy. But there must be partings, too. We cannot escape the Fates, my child.'

'Core . . . Core! Where are you?'

The bright poppies nodded in the golden field.

'Core!'

Then they exploded into a laughing scarlet storm as Core, goddess of the spring, flung herself fiercely into Demeter's arms, once more to be armisticed with kisses.

The world was in summer and the days were long. Demeter smiled, all disaster forgotten in her vast nature and love. Then the screech-owl hooted his tale of the pomegranate seeds and the harsh necessity of the Fates. It was time for Demeter and Core to part. Three long, dark months must Core stay with Hades. Three long, dark months must Demeter wander the world, calling her child in vain. 'Core . . . Core. . . .'

But she would come again. Great Rhea had promised. In spite of the Fates, each year Demeter's child would return.

16● A Charming Lad

It was in the days of Core. The world was green and the river nymphs, freed from ice, flashed laughing among the nearby thickets—only to fall into eager arms. Zeus, unchanging Zeus, seemed everywhere . . . as quail, swan, eagle, cloud and even as a shower of gold. His ceaseless, winged passion hovered, spied and pounced on the world below till it seemed to the careless nymphs that every bird and every gust of rain contained the god. Nor were the nymphs the only ones who looked askance at sudden changes in the weather. Mighty Hera watched with cloud-piercing eyes and divine anger as the great god littered the earth with Zeuslings. . . . But the day would come when even Zeus would be called to account. The queen of Heaven brooded in her lonely bedchamber, while laughter from below tinkled in the air as the nymphs tumbled like blown petals to a warm wind.

Mortal women, lacking the nymphs' lightness and speed, were more circumspect; they needed time for their passions to give them wings; they needed flattery and courtship. Such was Chione, a girl of high family who lived in Attica, between Eleusis and Athens.

She was very lovely, in a mortal fashion, and called to mind the disturbing beauty of Pandora. She wandered by the lilting streams—dreaming of lovers rather than with them.

From between the leaves the hot nymphs watched her, half-puzzled, half-pitying. When she bathed she kept to the shadows as if she were frightened by her own nakedness; and then walked on, closely gowned.

But Apollo had glimpsed her. No less than his almighty father, the sun-god was in love with love and often burned with more than his duty's fire. The foliage was nowhere thick enough to keep out his beams, and the god had peered through with abruptly kindled desire. The sun burned bright—and seemed to hurry as Apollo sped on to stable his fiery horses and be free to meet Chione on her own ground, in her own night.

Immortal Hermes had seen her too. In the shape of a crane he'd perched among the branches and had a closer, longer look.

'I saw her first!' shouted Apollo angrily, leaning from his blazing chariot while his unwatched horses pawed the high clouds and tossed them across the sky in golden shreds.

Hermes smiled and stared as Chione dried herself and put on her gown, tying the girdle firmly against the light-fingered breeze. Like his great brother and his great father, Hermes was a lover too . . . a lover with a sideways smile and an eye that twinkled with shrewd dreams. . . .

'She's for the arms of Apollo!' came the sun-god's voice, from farther in the west.

'And why not?' murmured Hermes, measuring the distance that his mighty brother had yet to go. 'But workaday gods must keep workaday hours—and wait till the night.'

So Chione, wandering on and dreaming of impossible lovers, met with a handsome shepherd who wore gold-coloured sandals that were ornamented with wings.

'Were I a god,' said this shepherd, accosting her, 'I would imprison you with the fire of my eyes and make you my goddess for an hour.'

Chione tossed her head and drew her gown close—for the shepherd's eyes did indeed burn bright.

'Were I a god,' pursued this shepherd, seeming to flicker into her path in a disturbing, uncanny way, 'I would make a green palace for you, under the trees, where nymphs would sing you love-songs and—'

'If you were a god,' interrupted Chione coldly, 'you would do these things instead of talking about them!'

So Hermes smiled—and did.

The sun-god's horses panted and dragged their chariot blazing down into the west. There was a distant thunder as the fiery wheels grumbled over the brazen floor of the stables . . . then quietness and night.

With mighty strides and still drenched with the golden

sweat of his labours, Apollo came.

'Brother,' said Hermes, flickering out of a thicket and meeting him by the stream. 'Has it not been rather a short day?' No one knows what tale Chione told to her proud Athenian father when she came home just before the next day's dawn. No one knows whether he believed it—or locked her up in a fury for the rest of that spring.

But when two sons were born to her, even the stern Athenian yielded a little. Not the hardest heart in the world could have resisted one of them: a bright-eyed, charming lad who could have wheedled the gold out of his grandfather's tooth. His name was Autolycus. . . .

Immortal Hermes, flying between Olympus and Parnassus, looked down on the tiny house by Athens. He smiled with unusual tenderness—and then sped on. The world below was in winter. Persephone was with her grim lover, Hades; and Demeter mourned while the screech owl cried. Great Zeus, turning from the frozen nymphs, cut a golden swathe through the daughters of men. Sometimes Hermes glimpsed him, blazing out of some maiden's bedchamber like a wayward star . . . and then he saw the maiden, all soft and amazed, leaning out into the night. Had it been a god, a dream, or a lover telling lies? Mighty Hera saw him too; and when morning came, the last night's love lay cold and dead, pierced by the feathered arrows of the virginal moon. Fierce Artemis, huntress and bringer of sudden death, had ranged herself beside the injured queen of Heaven whose desire for revenge was ever growing. . . .

Hermes frowned and longed for the coming of the spring; everywhere his sharp ears heard the busy clatter of the Fates as the cold days killed and killed.

But his Autolycus did not die. Instead, he grew into a sleek and handsome boy who left behind a trail of indulgent smiles that never quite knew what they'd smiled at when afterthought declared they should have frowned. Long and often the god lingered above the little house by Athens . . . and added yet another smile to young Autolycus's stock, till at last the great god of make-believe could contain himself no longer and went down to meet his charming son.

It was on a summer's day and the slippery child was walking by the banks of a certain stream when he met with a tall shepherd who wore golden sandals ornamented with wings.

Courteously Autolycus stepped aside; but the shepherd's courtesy coincided exactly with his own. They were still face to smiling face. Again Autolycus moved—and again they moved together. So Autolycus said, 'Sir, I will stand still. Pass whichever side you will.'

The shepherd looked him up and down; observed his neat limbs and thick dark curling hair. He nodded.

'Were I a god,' he said humorously, 'I'd be pleased to own such a son.'

'Were you a god, sir,' said young Autolycus, smiling sideways at the stream, 'I'd be pleased to own such a father.'

The shepherd turned his head to hide the laughter in his eyes. Then the boy, being, after all, a boy, picked up a stone and threw it in the stream, and knelt down to see what fish he'd flushed and whether they were worth catching. The shepherd watched him; then with a crinkled look at the sun, sat cross-legged beside him and helped by prodding the straining weeds with a long, ribboned staff. 'If I were a god,' he murmered idly to the racing stream, 'and I could do such things and change such things as they say gods can do, what would you like, Autolycus?'

The boy frowned and thought deeply. He was of the age when nothing surprised. Streams might turn to gold and nursery chairs become wild beasts, crouching at his feet. From time to time he turned his head—to find his sidelong glance met by the waiting shepherd's.

'Would you like to be loved, Autolycus?'

'I am,' said the boy honestly. 'People like me, you know.'

'Certainly you've inherited good looks—'

'And charm, too. Everyone agrees I have much charm. Also I'm musical. Already I can play the lyre and pipes.'

'Would you like to be modest, Autolycus? Would you like the gift of modesty?'

'Why, sir? What should I do with it?'

'Wear it as a cloak, Autolycus. It might save you from many a bitter wind.'

The boy shrugged his shoulders as if the shepherd's advice

was all very well, but for somebody else. The shepherd sighed. 'When old Prometheus made men and women, he gave them life but not much else besides. Every little helps. . . .'

'But that was a long time ago. They say the gods have helped since then. . . . Between you and me, sir,' said Autolycus, sitting back on his heels and eyeing the shepherd's quaint sandals, 'I'd hope for something better from a god than what I could do by myself. I *am* modest. Everyone says so. I'd sooner be rich, and—'

'And what, Autolycus?'

'—and not get caught.'

'How do you mean?' The shepherd glanced rapidly at the sky and then back to Autolycus with a mixture of brightness and suspicion.

'Well, sir—I've thought a lot about it. Palaces and kingdoms are all very well; but they're easily lost, or—or stolen. And unless you've the strength of a Titan, it's hard to hold on to what you've come by. You'd not believe it, but people round here, if so much as a cow is missing, track it down with sticks in their hands and murder in their hearts.'

Autolycus spoke with such feeling that the shepherd divined he spoke from experience, even though he was so young.

'Would you be a thief, then, Autolycus?'

'Did I say so, sir?'

'Would you be a thief like Sisyphus—that pigmy Prometheus with the manners of a brutish Ares?' pursued the shepherd.

'Sisyphus is rich,' said the boy enviously. 'And between you and me, he's no fool, sir.'

'It is not between you and me,' said the shepherd coldly. 'The world knows Sisyphus. The hoof marks of the herds he's stolen are like a trumpeting highway of tongues.'

'I'd have tied tree-bark to their hooves,' said the boy dreamily. 'Or something like that.'

The shepherd started—then shifted slightly as if to evade some sudden heat of the sun.

'I wish,' went on the boy in so low a voice that the shepherd bent near to hear him, 'I wish I could change the look of things so that anything I picked up, or found, or happened on, I could make look my own. For between you and me, sir—and it really is between you and me—that *would* be a gift of the gods;

especially for lads like me who are more peaceable and delicate than Titans—even though they dream as high.'

The talk of dreams appeared to have infected the shepherd; he lapsed into a brooding quiet. His golden eyes seemed to shed veils and mirror a wider world than the banks of the dancing little stream. Endless sands and landlocked pools of light that sparkled fierily.

'You've caught something!' said the boy suddenly.

The shepherd awoke from his dream. He laughed and drew his staff out of the coiling water. A fish jerked and twisted and flashed on the end of it. He gave it to Autolycus and in so doing touched the boy's head and hands with the strange staff.

'If I were truly a god and you were truly my son,' he murmured, 'I think I would grant you the gift of changing the look of things. . . .'

'And—?' said Autolycus, holding the fish by its tail and staring with childish desire at the shepherd's pretty sandals.

'And the modesty not to overstep the limits of your nature,' said the shepherd, abruptly standing up, 'and ask for too much.'

Then, with a curious, half-sideways, half-backwards movement, the shepherd vanished into the wood that skirted the stream.

The boy Autolycus gazed after him. 'If he was truly a god and I was truly his son,' he whispered to himself, 'I'd never get caught again.'

He grinned cheerfully and walked neatly by the stream, carrying the marvellous fish and the marvellous story home to Chione, his mother.

17● Two Thieves

The lands of Sisyphus straddled the Isthmus of Corinth.
Everything about him was huge; his strength, his wealth and
his villainy. His cattle were said to be as splendid as the
legendary herds of Apollo; and his brilliant wife, Merope, was
reputed to be a Titan's daughter. Nothing but the best for
mortal Sisyphus who, if he lacked fire, would have picked the
pocket of the sun.

Now Sisyphus, unlike the gods but like all other men, had a
neighbour. It was perhaps the one thing he had that hadn't
been stolen. He'd had neighbours before, but none like this
one whose charm and modesty were almost supernatural. His
name was Autolycus. Several times he'd called on Sisyphus
and admired the treasures of his home; but when he left,
Sisyphus counted them up with a shrewd frown.

There was something about this sleek, dark-haired neighbour, who always seemed to go through doors sideways, that
he didn't altogether trust. Under the perfume of scented oil
that wafted from his neat curls, Sisyphus was certain he'd
caught the familiar whiff of dishonesty.

But nothing was ever missing, so Sisyphus concluded he'd
frightened Autolycus off.

Nonetheless, Sisyphus kept a watchful eye across his wide
rolling pastures towards where Autolycus had built his modest
home on the shoulder of a hill.

It was in the spring time and Sisyphus's fields were sparkling
green. Indeed, they seemed to be greener than usual; or rather,
more green than usual seemed to be showing among his mighty
grazing herds. Sisyphus's eyes narrowed. Either his lands had
stretched or his cattle had dwindled.

He stared across the landscape towards the humble estate of

Autolycus—then back to his own gigantic domain. He did this at frequent and unexpected intervals, sometimes early in the morning and sometimes in the secret time of evening when the herds cast giant shadows like mountains on stilts.

There was no doubt. His cattle was steadily dwindling. Unfortunately, Autolycus's seemed to be increasing at almost the same rate. This was odd.

Savagely Sisyphus scowled at his own thinning pastures—and then towards his neighbour's crowded land. He scratched his head. Though his own cattle had been of a rich reddish brown, and Autolycus's were unarguably black and white, there was something familiar about them.

He shook his fist and, in the distance, Autolycus, perhaps mistaking the gesture, waved to him courteously and bowed.

Sisyphus nodded grimly. 'Very well, my oily friend. I don't know how you've done it, but I'll catch you at it yet. And then you'll wish you'd settled elsewhere and not matched your wits against great Sisyphus.'

That evening Sisyphus and his servants were busy among the engulfing shadows of his herds and, try as he might, Autolycus could not see what they were at. He could hear a faint sound of scraping and the occasional lowing of some protesting cow; but nothing more. He shrugged his shoulders and waited for the modesty of night.

Next morning, Autolycus received a visit. Sisyphus's servants called and sternly asked to see his cattle. Autolycus, all courtesy, said he understood his neighbour's herds were failing and he was very sorry on that account. No one liked to see cattle disappear. It was a sad and uncomfortable thing. But as Sisyphus's herds were horned and reddish-brown, and all his own were hornless and noticeably black-and-white, he didn't see how he could help. But he, Autolycus, was the last man to stand in the way of a just inquiry. By all means, search the stables and the fields. Better it should be done at once rather than that suspicion should be left to hang like a cloud between neighbours. An honest man has nothing to fear and welcomes further proof of his honesty. An honest man—

Autolycus stopped. His smile turned waxen and his complexion matched it. He opened his mouth and shut it; and looked exceedingly awkward. The servants of Sisyphus stared at him grimly. They pointed to the hoofs of a cow. There was something engraved on the inside.

Autolycus's mind flew back to the scraping he'd heard in the evening. He bent down to examine the tell-tale hoof, thinking furiously how it might be accounted for.

Alas! It was beyond even him. The trail of indulgent smiles that had followed him since childhood came to an abrupt end. On the inside of the cow's hoof were scored the damning words, 'Stolen by Autolycus.'

'Some god must have done it,' mumbled Autolycus feebly, observing Sisyphus's servants rummaging among other informative cows.

'Some god indeed,' came the stern reply. There was silence; and the great sun grinned down on the unlucky scene, making Autolycus sweat even more.

Suddenly there was a shriek from the front of the house. Autolycus, thankful for any excuse to escape, rushed to see what had happened.

He was too late. While the search had been going on at the back, Sisyphus had taken his revenge uninterrupted at the front. Autolycus saw his mighty neighbour departing, shaking with triumphant laughter. He had ravished Autolycus's daughter, Anticleia, and left her, scarlet-cheeked and sobbing, in the porch. Her gown was torn, her hair awry and everything about her proclaimed her ruin. Sisyphus had struck a frightful double blow.

Even as he bent to comfort Anticleia, whose shame was giving way to anger, Autolycus saw his cattle being driven across the fields.

'Avenge me, father,' wept the girl. 'For who will marry me now?'

Autolycus nodded. Sisyphus had certainly damaged his daughter's chances. He scowled and clenched his fists.

But Sisyphus was a big man, even a head taller than Autolycus; and he had the strength of a Titan. Autolycus relaxed his fists. He remembered the shepherd he'd met by the stream, long ago. 'Do not overstep the limits of your nature.' Well . . . well, there was no doubt that Sisyphus was outside the limits of his nature.

'Avenge me, father,' repeated Anticleia, her lovely face

cancelled with tears.

'Yes . . . yes . . .' muttered Autolycus, stroking his daughter's tangled hair and gazing mournfully towards where the huge figure of Sisyphus dwindled in the distance. 'Revenge.' He sighed. 'But what's done cannot be undone, my dear. Not that I don't feel a father's anger and sense of proper outrage. But— but were I to go and bring you back the head of monstrous Sisyphus, what good would it do? Maybe you'd bruise your little foot with kicking it—and then it would hang about and smell out the house. The sweetness of revenge, my child, very soon turns rotten and plagues the revenger. Surely, daughter, it is more a father's duty to look to the future?'

'What future?' wept Anticleia bitterly.

'We must not look on it,' said Autolycus, brightening up and exercising his divine gift for changing the appearance of things, 'as being the grievous loss of your honour. Let us instead look on it as it truly is. He has lost in you his child. He shall have no part of the infant you will bear. It will be a son, Anticleia; I know it . . . and glorious. Yes, indeed, we have robbed Sisyphus of a real treasure.' Autolycus grew more and more enthusiastic as he changed disaster into triumph—and hoped his daughter would see it the same way, too. 'I know a prince,' he went on, effortlessly. 'A gentle, simple fellow called Laertes. Ithaca is his home. You shall marry him, Anticleia; and all that's happened this morning will remain forever between you and me. Laertes shall be the father of my grandson. . . .'

'Is this, then, to be your only revenge, father,' whispered Anticleia wearily, 'to have deceived the prince of Ithaca?'

'Pooh!' said Autolycus. 'Laertes will never suspect.'

'I would have thought,' said Anticleia softly, 'that the grandson of Autolycus and the son of Sisyphus would rouse suspicion in a daisy.'

'He will bring us glory,' mused Autolycus, lapsing into golden dreams. 'His fame will blot out Sisyphus as if he'd never been. And that will be a true revenge, my daughter.' Here he smiled as he deftly shifted all thought of vengeance onto the unborn shoulders. 'Call him the Angry One, Anticleia. For my sake, call him Odysseus. . . .'

Prince Laertes was everything that Autolycus had represented him to be—at least in the way of simplicity. He married Anticleia and, in the course of time and nature, the child was born on stony Ithaca. Proudly Laertes claimed fatherhood; while Anticleia smiled a trifle sadly and called the boy Odysseus.

Then she returned to watching over the darkly winking sea for the next tall ship to come from Corinth with the news she longed to hear . . . that someone had avenged her on that great villain, Sisyphus.

But the world was Sisyphus's garden, and Autolycus was his footstool. The huge criminal seemed to get great pleasure from jeering at the gentle thief, and lost no opportunity of belittling him. Merope, his proud wife, irritably begged him not to make a fool of himself by breathing fire that scorched no more than the air. Autolycus wasn't worth it. But Sisyphus had got it into his head that Autolycus had been helped by a god, and he longed to sting the oily fellow into admitting it so that the world might know that Sisyphus had outwitted a thief who was half divine.

At last, Merope, hoping to turn her great husband's ambition towards something nobler, told him in confidence that Atlas was her father. At once, Sisyphus claimed Prometheus as an uncle by marriage and began to entertain powerful and confused thoughts of inheriting the Titan's vast estate.

'He is going mad,' wrote Autolycus to his daughter in Ithaca. 'Between ourselves, I do believe our friend will try to outwit Zeus himself. If so, then I fear that vengeance is entirely out of my hands. So watch the sky, daughter. . . .'

He sent also a jar of perfumed oil for his grandson Odysseus's rich gold hair. Then he continued to watch with interest the gigantic affairs of his neighbour, while helping himself to odds and ends of cattle from the other side.

18● A Deadly Vision

It was late in the year and the last of autumn lingered in the air. Already Demeter had lost her child and the river nymphs cast frightened glances in their fathers' streams, seeing in them the menace of ice. But Zeus still played, for the game of the year was not yet done. He came in gold—as if to tempt the woods and glades into an unseasonable spring . . . while mighty Hera watched and bided her gigantic time. Sometimes, in the deepest part of the night, the great goddess would whisper to the nodding sea; sometimes in the blinding blaze of noon, she would move across the sun . . . and, as always, the terrible arrows of Artemis would strike wherever wild Zeus loved. Such an autumn was in the air. . . .

Dreamily great Sisyphus watched the brown leaves curl and twist away from an oak tree that stood at the edge of a wood he'd newly claimed. He played Titanic games in his mind: if such a leaf fell before another, then he would gain this and that; if they fell together, he would live a hundred years more. Whichever way they fell, he could not lose.

Then, quite suddenly, there came a rustling and a whispering as a breeze sprang up and fidgeted all the crisp dry foliage in the wood. Sisyphus frowned, and with humorous daring wagered possession of the world itself on the fall of a single trembling leaf. The breeze grew stronger. A little whirlwind seemed to have lost its way among the trees. A column of leaves was spinning and dancing as if to get out; then all at once it did, and with a flash of red and gold and brown, it cleaned the oak tree as if with a broom. He thought he heard a cry. He felt the air grow warm—like an unseasonable spring—and there was a smell of honey everywhere. He crouched down in the long grass and watched the whirlwind struggle in the naked branches of the oak.

Then came a gust of rain . . . from nowhere, for the sky was clear. It beat down the dancing leaves. The air sparkled and Sisyphus fancied he saw two vast bright forms struggling in passion and dread. Even as he watched, he saw the brighter, grander shape bear the other backwards.

He saw two faces—one fiery, one amazed. He saw the oak tree quiver and heard it crack from the unearthly heat. . . .

Birds screamed and shrieked and spiralled wildly into the sky; then down they plunged to scorch their feathers in the blazing air. They were sparrows, mad little sparrows. . . .

The double fire grew brighter, leaping and twisting in the air till all the grass and trees and rocks were tipped with melted gold.

Sisyphus's eyeballs were blistering—but yet he watched, dimly understanding the stupendous scene. Suddenly, the radiance grew to an intolerable proportion so that the very air moaned. For an instant, it remained thus; then the heat diminished and the smell of honey redoubled, flooding the air and drowning the senses in the space of a second.

A golden man and woman—of rippling, uncertain outline— seemed to be lying in the grass. Slowly Sisyphus grinned as the wonder resolved itself. Here was a god and nymph in ecstasy. He had seen it—he had seen it!

But there was more to come. The nymph slipped from the embrace and fled. The golden man started and with new desire began to pursue her. They flickered among the trees, flaring out from time to time, leaving a fiery imprint on Sisyphus's eyes so that he was half-blinded by a multi-coloured image of laughter that engulfed the world.

Faster and faster burned the pursuit—arms like flames licked round the shaking trees; then, abruptly, it stopped.

A new sound was in the air, a rushing, roaring sound. The nymph vanished and the golden man stood listening with a blazing smile, half mocking, half angry.

Sisyphus trembled in the long grass as the savage uproar grew nearer. The trees swayed and the lower branches splintered away from the trunks with loud cracks like volleying thunderbolts. Water began to pour through the wood like silver blood from a thousand wounds. There was a stench of weed and slime and the golden man flashed from tree to tree, shaking with laughter.

Now it was he who was being pursued, and suddenly Sisyphus saw the pursuer. He caught his breath.

Robed in his torrent like a drowned dream of stony eyes, mouth, hair and hands, came mighty Asopus—the god of the river—and straightway there began a chase of gigantic dimensions. The river god blundered through the wood, uprooting the stout trees and flinging them aside so that their roots made snaky bushes with forking, earth-clogged tongues, while the golden man, still helpless with angry laughter, twisted endlessly out of his reach.

The wood was full of reflections as the river god rushed and plunged. Strange skies appeared amid the falling trees; and upside-down mountains and slanting palaces whose porticos broke into ripples and flowed into the ground. Then Sisyphus glimpsed himself, thin-eyed and ambitious, peering secretly into the uncanny flood.

The god had seen him. Sisyphus shrank back; then, trembling, stood erect and stared up while his narrow head was bursting to control the vision.

Asopus paused between two lofty pine trees, his huge limbs greenly glimmering; above them, reflected clouds sailed across his stony face so that his cold eyes seemed continually veiled and unveiled by billowing cataracts, while his cheeks were scarred with deep, tree-filled ravines whose other selves plunged through mountains far, far in the north.

'My daughter,' whispered the god. 'Where is she? Where did she fly?'

Sisyphus's mind struggled to stretch the limits of his mortal brain. He panted with exultation; he was poised between gods. He had spied through his grass keyhole on a divine secret; and now his power was enormous.

'I saw her ravished,' he answered the terrible green god, who seemed the larger of the two and consequently would have the more to offer.

'Where is he, the ravisher?'

Sisyphus turned. He saw the golden man, crouching beyond the oak. Eyes like suns burned into his own: there was an extraordinary and horrible rage in them. Then they softened into a strange amusement and the golden man lifted a secret finger to his lips. 'Be silent, Sisyphus.'

'Where, Sisyphus?'

'Give me a spring, great Asopus, to enrich my land. Give me an eternal spring and I'll tell you—'

Even as greedy Sisyphus spoke, there came a gentle rushing sound from near at hand. Water was sobbing and dancing out of the ground. It winked and twinkled as the lively bubbles jostled round the dry grass. . . .

'There,' said Sisyphus, pointing to the oak, 'your daughter's ravisher is there.' He approached the concealment and, with shaking hands, drew aside the thick tall grass.

Huge and still, there lay before him nothing but a stone. It was round—shaped vaguely like a giant's face which stared up to the autumn sky from whence it took a mocking gleam of gold. A stone. . . .

The river god had gone and nothing remained of the wild vision but the tattered wood, the scorched grass and a lingering smell of weeds and honey. But the spring still bubbled and Sisyphus, enmeshed in the web of eternity, turned slowly back towards his mansion while the round stone seemed to watch after him with a quietly vengeful air.

When he had departed, the stone dissolved back into the golden god. It was Zeus. He rose into the sky with a glare that eclipsed the sun. The gods on high Olympus shrank away before his fury. Hera alone looked on—and her smile was as menacing as the great god's frown.

She saw her vast husband gather in his murderous artillery to vent his rage upon the ancient river god who had pursued him; she heard him whisper down the cleft of Tartarus, bidding dread Hades himself to take the wretched man who'd spied on his lust. 'Take him, brother—now!'

Then she left him, and in her black and scarlet gown leaned across the sky and whispered dangerously to the sun, the moon and the impatient mounting sea.

19● The Battle with Death

The sky above Corinth and as far away as Ithaca was red as blood; but to Sisyphus it was no more than the gentle blush of evening. He was caught beyond escape in the divine net. His great mansion, pillared against the sky, seemed shrunk and humble, and in his mind he raised towers as high as the sun. Labourers in his fields seemed to him like tiny insects, scurrying after his countless herds; and even the heavy beasts were like flies on a green table that had suddenly become too small for mighty Sisyphus.

Such was the state to which this powerful man had been brought that he dipped his head as he passed under his own high portico, for his thoughts brushed the sky. The vision in the wood had blasted him and cracked his mould, letting in everywhere too loud a laughter and too bright a light.

He never heard the unearthly thunder of gigantic horses' hooves, nor the roar of a dreadful chariot as it split the paved ground and hurled the huge engraved stones aside as if they'd been no more than autumn leaves. The screams and shrieks of his servants as they fled from the tottering house, and even the whimpering of Merope, moved him no more than the squeaking of mice. What was mortal terror to a man who'd spied on a secret of the gods?

Dreamily he stared into implacable eyes and wondered, almost idly, who was this huge dark personage standing before him who'd scattered his household and put out the lights?

Sisyphus smiled cunningly. It was Autolycus's doing—some crazy illusion of that oily thief. But the man who'd talked with a river god was not to be taken in by shadows.

Then the enormous shadow whispered, 'Sisyphus, you are finished now. Sisyphus, you are dead.' Dull fires gleamed in the pits of its eyes; but they were fires without heat. Grim Hades held out his iron hands and Sisyphus saw the fatal manacle. It was a brazen serpent of terrible beauty. Misshapen Hephaestus had made it as a wedding gift; its jaws were set agape, and once they were shut there was no undoing them till the imprisoned flesh withered and the bone flaked into dust.

A chill crept over Sisyphus's heart and the heat of his vision waned. Was he then but an ordinary man face to face with the most hated god in the universe? Was this his end and was he, after all he'd done and all he'd seen, to vanish from the world as if he'd never been?

'Give me your hands.'

Then great Sisyphus, watcher of the gods, fell to his knees and began to howl and shriek for mercy. He beat the stone floor and begged for another month, another week, another day. He wept that it was for Merope's sake, for his children's sake. . . . He sobbed to see the sun once more—to hear the birds and smell the autumn flowers that grew unheeded outside his bedchamber and now seemed the richest of all his possessions.

'Give me your hands.'

'Another hour, great god! Please—please—*please*!'

The Titan by marriage began to crawl backwards as the terrible god advanced. He scuttled like a frightened pig, squealing and grunting as it sees the slaughterer's knife in the hand that has always carried food.

'Five minutes!'

'Sisyphus, my lord!' moaned Merope. 'There's no escaping. Let me remember you with dignity—'

The doomed man howled with rage and bit her leg for daring to live on after he was gone. Then, of a sudden, Merope's words seemed to take effect. Sisyphus grew calm. He knelt and stared almost wistfully at the brazen serpent that now cast its thin shadow across his wrists. He smiled—and Merope wept afresh. His little eyes blinked up trustingly at the huge god.

'Such a little thing,' he murmured, as might a child.

'It will fit you, Sisyphus.'

'Would it fit Autolycus? Would it catch so slippery a pair of wrists as his? Let me see it, great god—let me touch it. How beautiful it is! Ah! it is cold. . . .'

Sisyphus, childlike Sisyphus, prattled on eagerly—and all the while his small wet eyes blinked up at the relentless god. But grim Hades, like all his eternal race, was of divine essence, unmixed with pity or any of the tangled dreams of the tragic creatures of Prometheus. His dealings were with the hopeless dead; the living and their fragile ways were strangers to him. Their movements were so small and brittle; their hands moved like darting dragonflies, here, there, everywhere. . . .

'Farewell, Merope, my love,' chattered Sisyphus. 'Farewell my children, farewell my home, my world, and—and—*farewell death*!'

Sisyphus's voice rose to a shriek as the brazen serpent snapped its jaws. It was not for nothing that Sisyphus's hands had spent their life in and out of other men's pockets. They had gained, apart from wealth, some deftness and speed. Thus the brazen serpent, in all its thin cold strength, encircled now the mighty wrists of grim Hades himself!

The gods looked down and shuddered at the frantic ambition of the man who'd spied on the secret lust of Zeus and laid his hands on eternity. Their estate was threatened; shadows gathered in the universe. Huge beings began to move and, in passing, extinguished the betraying stars. They looked to Zeus, whose lust and fury had brought on the disaster; but the lord of the sky had eyes only for his enemy, the river god. Then they looked to the terrible queen of Heaven who beckoned to the sun, the moon and the sea. . . .

Now began the strange triumph of Sisyphus of Corinth who had imprisoned the god of the dead.

He roared, he shouted, he danced, he flew out into his fields and laughed as his herds lowed and lumbered away amazed. He sent huge proclamations shrieking on the wings of the wind so that all might know that Sisyphus had conquered the lord of the dead.

Men rose from death-beds—old men, young men, worn-down grandmothers creaked out and blinked—and tottered back into the fierce quarrels of life. Dying kings reached out for sceptres already handed over, and eager sons whipped fingers back from near inheritances as if they'd been burned. Murderers fled

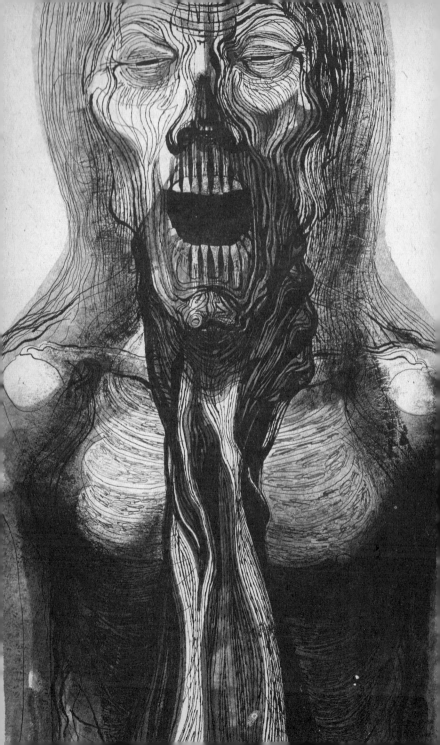

from victims unkilled; and those who'd shrewdly made their last peace, found themselves nudged sharply back to war.

War! But it was war without end as maimed remnants laid about them with stout right arms, chopped from the shoulder and brandished in the left. And everywhere mankind heaved and struggled under the monstrous burden of an immortality for which they'd not been fashioned.

And all the while, in the midst of this convulsion in nature, the mansion of Sisyphus in Corinth rocked and shuddered as the vast god within struggled against the brazen serpent. But Hephaestus's work was eternal—and Hades could only pit the divine strength of his left hand against the equal strength of his right.

All had fled the house and scarcely dared look back at its bulk—now of an unnatural blackness and quaking like some gigantic beast against the sky. Sisyphus alone remained and jeered with ferocious glee at his dreadful prisoner. 'Behold mighty Sisyphus!' he howled triumphantly. 'Saviour of the world! Now we'll inherit it! Now we're on a level with the gods!'

Suddenly the mansion cracked. The pillars clenched and the great roof fell thunderously in. For a moment the huge shape of Hades was seen, black as night under the noonday sky. Men in the fields many miles away saw him and flung themselves to the ground. The air was full of fire and the clash of armour, and the serpent round the grim god's wrists snapped.

Ares, murderous child of Hera, had struck it with his spear. The god of war had come to free the god of the dead.

Then Ares laughed and sent his brazen shout echoing across the crawling battlefields; he had restored the chief prize of war, which was death.

Sisyphus staggered wildly this way and that. But not for long. Hades took him—seized him by his knotted neck.

He shrieked violently and fought. Then he saw Merope watching in pity and dread.

'Do not bury me! Do not hide me in the earth! I will be back—I will be back!'

But his raging spirit vanished in the thick clouds of disaster and his cries were overwhelmed by the thunder of the gigantic horses' hooves.

She mourned him, sinister villain though he'd been; he was her husband and Merope had her pride. Servants washed his battered face, and set his shouting lips at rest.

Autolycus came to pay his respects; stared down cautiously at the dead man's closed eyes—and offered to help the widow with the disposal of unwanted effects.

Then, on the morning of the third day, before Merope's appalled gaze, Sisyphus came back. His dead eyes opened into crafty slits and his dead mouth stretched into a cunning smile.

He sat up. His hair was white, his skin was of a leaden grey; but he had come back.

He held a bandaged finger to his lips, chuckled and coughed to expel the dust of death that had settled in his throat. Not even the immortal gods could keep Sisyphus down. He chuckled again—and his little eyes flickered merrily behind the corpse film that partly dulled them. Great Persephone had let him go. He had explained to her, honourably and openly, that he hadn't been buried. He had been taken without warning, without time to make his peace. . . . He would rot neglected under the sky and be hideous in the golden corn, like a black corrupted poppy. . . . Again he coughed, for some scraps of dust were in his lungs. So Demeter's child had given him three days. . . .

'Three days?' whispered Merope. 'What can we do in three short days?'

Sisyphus looked at his wife in astonishment. 'Do you take me for a fool? Do you think I mean to keep my word? When have I ever done such a thing before? He-he! The gods will have to look sharp indeed if they want to catch Sisyphus! Why, Autolycus! What d'you want?' Sisyphus looked up. A figure was standing beside him and watching him with a curious sideways smile. Sisyphus tugged at his winding sheet which was tight about his chest. 'Had you come thieving, Autolycus? Then think again, my friend. Sisyphus is back. He-he! Sisyphus has cheated death for a second time!'

The figure moved. It lifted a golden staff that fluttered white ribbons. It stepped lightly and its feet came close to Sisyphus's eyes. They wore curious golden sandals ornamented with wings. . . .

'Autolycus—?'

'It is not Autolycus, my friend.'

'Then—?'

'I am Hermes. Come, Sisyphus. You may cheat the god of the dead; but you cannot cheat the god of illusion. I am stronger than Hades, my friend.'

Immortal Hermes took Sisyphus by the hand in a grip there was no undoing and Sisyphus groaned and wept his farewell to the world for the last time.

His servants buried him in a hole by the wood where he'd seen the vision. Then they filled it in and proud Merope looked for the great round stone that Sisyphus had spoken of, but it had vanished; so she smoothed the earth that none should ever find the great criminal's grave and dishonour it.

'Our friend is dead at last,' wrote Autolycus to his daughter in rocky Ithaca. 'He went with a great commotion—but he went in the end. Now he is at peace—'

In cold, bleak Tartarus, beyond the dreary Fields of Asphodel, there rises a black hill whose steep sides are channelled with wear. From here comes a tiny screaming as a figure, seeming no larger than a beetle, heaves and pushes a great round stone that glints with a mockery of gold. He is trying to push it to the top of the hill, but each time it reaches almost to the summit, its terrible weight overwhelms him and it thunders silently back into the valley in clouds of choking dust; then the tiny figure screams his despair and goes back to begin again. Neither hope nor dreams can sustain him; his labour is doomed and eternal. Though he knows he must fail, he cannot stop. He pushes and pushes to a summit that is not there, and the great round stone gleams mockingly like a sun that is anchored in the night. Will the dawn come this time? Nearly . . . nearly. . . .

'A—ah! Let me die!' shrieks the ghost as the stone overwhelms him, as it always must.

Such is the peace of Sisyphus—who betrayed a secret of almighty Zeus.

'But enough of Sisyphus,' went on Autolycus to his daughter in distant Ithaca. 'Merope has vanished from Corinth, and you'd scarce recognize their fine mansion now. It is going to wrack and ruin. . . .'

By the same tall ship he sent also several choice goblets and a chest of crystal bowls to be laid up for his grandson Odysseus—as an heirloom, so to speak, from his departed father. . . .

But the vessel bearing the gifts and the news was delayed by storms. Furious winds raged across the sea and the waves stood up like ragged mountain ranges, boiling with snow.

Patiently Anticleia waited, and watched the strange configurations of cloud that swirled in the sky.

20 ● The Second Fall

The eye of the tempest was over Corinth. It glared down with livid anger and turned the wide landscape to a silvered lead. Something was amiss in nature; the heavens were awry. Men prayed frantically to be forgiven their secret sins and mothers hurried their children to the tops of houses, remembering tales of the ancient flood.

Whips of lightning lashed and struck again and again at the winding river Asopus—as if to scourge the god in his bed. Flaming rocks and white-hot stones flew like pelting stars and hissed into the trembling water. Vainly the river fled before the unnatural onslaught, dragging at its very source to escape. It foamed, it roared, it leaped its banks; and wherever the straining reeds parted the stony eyes of the god stared up in helpless agony as raging Zeus took aim to burn them out.

Savage beyond measure, the great god was hurling his vengeance down on his last nymph's father—the interrupter of his necessary lust. It was this pent-up energy that now flowered into a spring to kill all summers. Through night and day the fire-storm fell, till the waters boiled and snarled. The reflections were all of flight and weird terror. Groups of villagers fled—flaring from every limb, then vanishing in thick red smoke; ravines and forests shivered into flaming fragments that danced across the mirrored eye of the extraordinary storm.

Here and there, between wild clouds, wandered the frightened sun, all pale and lustreless as if it had been unharnessed and abandoned; and dwellers by the sea saw terrible Poseidon rise in a shaking mountain of dark water to overwhelm the sky.

A shadow fell across the back of avenging Zeus as he crouched over the ramparts of high Olympus; but he was fixed in his fury and did not feel it. Ceaselessly his huge arms made crooked lightnings over Corinth as he pelted the writhing river god with his fire, and brushed aside the congregating clouds whenever they hid Asopus's agony. The river was burning down all its length—it was bleeding with fire like some dreadful running wound in the earth's flesh. Beside such gigantic rage the gods themselves were but as masterless mice; and blazing Zeus paid no heed to the drifting abandoned sun, the mountain in the sea nor the empty husk of the moon.

A second shadow crossed his golden back, and the glittering, all-killing thunderbolt that lay at his side moved subtly out of reach. . . . Then a third shadow came, a queer, intricate netting with a hundred nodding ends. It began to lift and lift till, for a moment, all the sky seemed to be made of hanging squares. And then—it struck!

There was a roar of thunder and all the corridors of the universe rattled and shook. Some part of the sky's fabric cracked, and an uncanny ashy dust drifted down to the world below, settling on treetops and spotting the surface of the sea. Then there was a silence; the storm ceased, the tempest's eye was quenched and the sky was suddenly emptied. All living things looked up aghast. The great god had fallen; Zeus had been overthrown. At last it had happened—even as it had happened to Cronus, near the world's beginning.

He lay by the Olympian ramparts, enmeshed in a divine net. A hundred knots secured it, so tied that none could be undone without its nine and ninety neighbours. He was bound by the thongs of eternity, whose ends were all beginnings to deeper, tighter tangles that bit into his limbs. He lifted up his mighty head and stared at his triumphant enemies.

Poseidon looked down on him, snarling with the greed that had ever consumed him. Apollo looked down on him—proud Apollo whose sun-chariot had inflamed ambition to rule where he rode. Artemis looked down on him—cold, angry Artemis whose virginal eyes had watched his rapes and ravishings even in her sacred groves. Demeter looked down on him—wild bereaved Demeter whose child he'd given to Hades. Even Athene was among them—wise Athene, born from his own head. Her fathomless eyes condemned him for the cruelty in nature that made all creation suffer for his lusts.

And towering above them all in her robes of scarlet and black was the queen of Heaven herself; mighty Hera whose terrible smile was the most menacing thing in the sky. Tormented pride had brought her at last to this gigantic revenge.

Far below in Tartarus, amid smoke-veiled cliffs of jet, the shackled Titans raised their ancient heads in hope of freedom, now that cruel Zeus was overthrown. Great Atlas, sunk in stone, groaned and dreamed of pardon; only Prometheus, bleeding in the Caucasian snow, was not deceived by hope; and far away, on the isle where Zeus's last nymph had fled, a serpent laid an egg in a stream and presently, snakes in their thousands wriggled across the land and poisoned it. Already one tyranny was replacing another. . . . Hera's vengeance was as harsh as Zeus's.

'Which of you?' whispered Zeus, his vast limbs straining against the thongs. He stared from one to another so that even the rebellious Olympians shuddered under his gaze. *'Which of you?'*

Hermes alone was not to be seen; for that immortal politician had not yet determined which way was his. Such was his respect and admiration for all the gods that he could not—in fairness to himself—declare his allegiance till he knew for certain who had won.

He had taken refuge under the discreet sea—even in the quiet grotto of Thetis and Eurynome; and there he waited patiently for the outcome of the great affair.

Interestedly he gazed round the rocky walls and admired the lovely trifles of Hephaestus's childhood works. From time to time he stopped and listened—as if awaiting a summons; but there was no sound save the wild music of the water foaming through the conch shell at the grotto's gate. He peered through the crystal window, but the green was empty and dark. All life, mortal and divine, was hiding from the revolution in the sky.

Then Thetis rose. Her glorious face was shadowed with fear. She drew her robe about her and bowed her head so none might divine her purpose from her eyes. Then, with a sudden flash of her silver sandals, which seemed to dance like two sea-creatures, she fled from the grotto.

Hermes shrugged his gleaming shoulders and returned to the crystal window and watched as the goddess, robed in her storm of bubbles, sped through the engulfing green, till at last she was lost and the underwater forests swayed back and hid the path she'd taken.

On and on rushed Thetis, her gentle spirit plunged into dismay. Dreams, terrible dreams, filled her immortal mind; memories of the dark tales told to Hephaestus, long ago. Gigantic murders and Fury-haunted nights; mad wars that scarred the heavens and smashed the stars—and Chaos creeping back like a huge black sea. . . .

She reached the ocean's edge; but still she sped on, and such was her wild haste that she seemed for a moment like an outstretched finger of the sea itself—till the joining water dropped away in the air and left her, like some speeding arrow's tip, all silver with fear.

She fled through the grove of black poplars and drew her mantle over her head. She was entering the dread realms of Tartarus, where the gentle goddess had never been but in her dreams.

She dared not look down, and tried to shut out the tiny screams and shrieks that filled the air like the high squeaking of unseen bats.

At last she came to the most dreaded place of all. Bewildered, she saw the towering cliffs of jet where the ruined Titans hung in the chains that had once held the Cyclopes. The sweat that ran eternally off their huge confined limbs had worn deep channels in the steep black walls, from whence it had run a little way to pool and dry in hillocks of salty crusts.

But it was not for the Titans she'd voyaged so far—and she turned aside from their tremendous pleading eyes. It was for one she knew by name alone—and whose gigantic shape she now saw moving amid the vapours that rose uneasily from the depths of the ravine.

'Briareus!' she called. 'Briareus! Come quickly—'
There was a whirlwind in the sky, a whirlwind with a hundred flailing arms. It had risen from beside the ocean and moved with unimagined speed across the heavens and towards the

silent battlements of Olympus.

Briareus, the hundred-handed giant, had come from Tartarus at the bidding of the goddess from the sea. Older than Zeus, older far than all the gods, he turned his tangled eyes wearily towards the ramparts and then, with his thousand twining fingers, reached for the deep knots that secured the lord of the sky. . . .

In the great council chamber the triumphant gods debated, and, with piercing ambition, glanced from time to time at the empty throne that stood above them all.

Then each looked to the others, and all threatened the first to move. Only Athene sat in silence; and her beloved owl crouched on her shoulder, its marvellous eyes extinguished in feathers of dismay. Beyond the casements the drifting sun and moon still wandered in the vacant sky.

Murderous Ares alone was grinning as he clashed from god to god and urged the joyous frenzy of universal war. Such was the gift of Ares that he seemed mad and savage only when he was on the other side; his hot breath in the ear was always the whisper of a divine god.

Suddenly a dangerous brightness seemed to flood the hall. Gods in mid-course stopped and stared at one another, bewildered that their radiance was dimmed.

'Which of you?'

They turned. In the doorway, his terrible golden head scarce clearing the high, engraved lintel-piece, stood eternal Zeus, god of the all-killing thunderbolt and lord of the sky. He had been freed!.

The gods shrank back, each into his little throne. They trembled, and the immortal mountain itself seemed to tremble with them as if it would crack into fragments and rush into the sea.

'Which of you?'

The bright gilding of their limbs dulled and tarnished before the advancing blaze. Then Hera started up and met him in his path. Though her power was shattered, her great pride was not.

'I was the one, dread Zeus. Who else but mighty Hera would have dared?'

He hung her in the sky with golden bracelets from her wrists and golden anvils to drag her ankles down. Hers was a royal fate. Her raging beauty stared down on the world, while her rich black hair flew across the face of the shaken moon. Stars pricked her fingertips, but such was the scope of her pride that she scorned to clench her hands and wore the stars like sharply splintered jewels; while in the northern sky her black and scarlet gown hung down in deep, unmoving folds. There she remained until Zeus's anger was spent.

Poseidon and Apollo, Zeus humbled in a lesser way. He sent them as bond-slaves to the world below and condemned them to labour—Poseidon by day and Apollo by night—to build a city for a king. Yet even as they raised the first huge stones, Zeus doomed the city to destruction so they knew they laboured in vain. They built the towers and morticed the walls and engraved the bronze floors—and ever knew that they were building the ghost of ruins. The city's name was Troy.

Such were the punishments of Zeus; the other gods he pardoned—all save one.

Hephaestus, ugly Hephaestus, stared out at the hanging lady in the sky. His scorched and sunken eyes were crinkled with looking, and his face, blackened with the heat of his forge, was furrowed with memories of pain.

He shambled back and forth, now looking out, now looking rapidly at his vast father who was brooding in an unearthly calm.

Sombrely he remembered how he had suffered from the pride of Hera—and how the lust for revenge had burned in his breast. He remembered the dark years in the grotto and how he had spent his savagery on bronze and gold, twisting it and hammering it till sweat blinded his eyes and he could do no more. Then he remembered how the object of his hatred—this same mighty lady who was stretched across the heavens—had given him her hand and helped him back, because she admired and wanted what he had done.

In that instant, anger left him and his strange heart had flooded with joy. In that instant he had become truly a god.

He hobbled to his father, squinting hideously, for Zeus's fire ever oppressed him.

'You are the eternal savage, great son of Cronus,' he muttered bitterly. 'You alone will never change. . . .'

Zeus stared down at his misshapen son. For a moment he seemed not to have heard. There was almost a smile on his lips. Then suddenly he leaned forward like some murderous flame that leaps out of a quiet fire and threatens the hearth with instant ruin.

With dreadful swiftness he seized the amazed Hephaestus by the foot.

'Go!' raged wild Zeus. 'Vile, twisted thing! For a second time, begone!'

Then, with all the strength of his gigantic arm, he hurled Hephaestus out into the frightened sky.

Such was the force with which he'd been flung that his path through the sky was at first upwards, before it began to plunge, so that it seemed that some great engraver had sketched a flaming arch in the heavens with a tool that writhed and twisted as it burned its way. High birds, crossing this path, shook and toppled as their wings were wrenched by a harsh roaring that streamed up from the blazing thing below.

The god howled as he fell; but this time it was not the crying of a fiery infant, it was the wild, weird howling of the knowledge of pain. There was no gentle goddess to raise her white arms from the sea to save him; he was for the hard, stony earth.

Far, far below he saw it, whirling and rushing to meet him as he screamed. Fields, rivers, seas and mountains twisted themselves into a great round—then, as his eyes rolled wildly, all the colours flew out into separate strands and patches of brown, green and silver, as loose and aimless as the tumbled threads left by the shears of the Fates.

Hephaestus squealed with terror and beat his powerful, blackened arms as if to fly; but he only twisted faster in the air and the loose patchwork below whirled back into its plaited round, bound in at its edges by the endless, looping sea.

It was like a shield—a gigantic shield, rimmed with hammered silver in a great pattern of waves. Forgetful of his agony, the god's mouth gaped and his starting eyes took in the intricate splendour of the design, in its spacious elements and in its glorious shape.

Here a proud river flowed, reflecting the sun till it was a fine seam of gold running between enamelled fields and through valleys of red and green bronze. Two cities of a pearly whiteness rose a hand's breadth apart. It seemed they'd been at war, and now their differences were resolved, for a stately procession in tiny jewelled colours moved from each towards the other, under high curled pennants of peace. What were they like, these pennants? They reminded him of something, long ago. Yes . . . yes. The falling god's eyes misted over as he remembered' the patterns of sea-shells that had once delighted him in Thetis's grotto. The pale pennants were curiously like them. . . .

'A shield,' he muttered. 'I must make a shield—'

Then he looked down again and saw that all had changed into a vast, engulfing green. At immense speed the world was rushing to meet him and, with a last tremendous shriek, Hephaestus struck it.

Like a flaming meteor torn from the sun, he had fallen from early morning till the edge of the night; now at last he crashed in shattered agony among the forests of the isle of Lemnos.

They found him moaning and whimpering in the ruins of a forest. The tall trees round about had been smashed by the violence of his descent, and here and there thin branches still flared and flickered.

At first, the islanders were frightened, and peered at the gleaming monstrous being from a distance; then, seeing him helpless, they approached and timidly offered him food and drink. Both his legs were broken and his immortal spirit seemed shattered beyond repair. He stared almost unseeingly at the frail creatures of Prometheus as they bothered him with their gentle care.

Like his mighty father but yesterday, he too was bound with a hundred knots of pain. What would they do with him? What would they want of him? How would they use their triumph over a fallen god?

They tried to mend his legs but, failing this, they brought straw and rushes and such soothing ointments as they knew. He was their guest, and to a guest they gave.

How long he lay there is not surely known. Certainly, it was

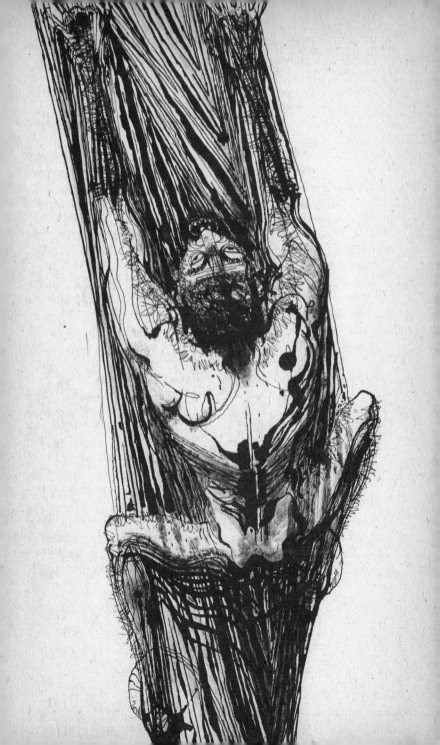

for several days and nights; for sailors passing the island of an evening noted with bewilderment the strange rich glow that seemed to come from its heart.

Then the god departed and dragged his useless legs across the weary way back to Olympus, leaving deep channels and twisted grooves where the ground was soft enough to take the imprint of his feet.

Up and up he climbed, never pausing though the agony was intense; sometimes dragging by his fingers alone, sometimes moving more swiftly where he obtained the leverage of his powerful arms. So great Hephaestus climbed towards the sky which was his home.

'A shield!' he panted, as if to sustain himself with the memory. 'I must make a shield. . . . Such a shield! . . . Yes, yes—a shield. . . .

At last the ramparts of Olympus reared before him, and as before a hand reached out to help him in. The god looked up. Hermes was there.

'Come, brother,' murmured the god of illusion with his sideways smile. 'Between you and me, eh? It is always between you and me.'

Hephaestus took his hand and nodded. Then he turned back and the two great brothers silently regarded the world. Their hands were still clasped, and for many minutes they remained thus, with their backs to Olympus and their faces towards mankind; the artificer in gold and bronze and the artificer in dreams.

'The weather is better now,' wrote Autolycus to his daughter in rocky Ithaca. 'All is busy and prosperous again. They say a new city is being built, and that it will be the most wonderful in the world. Certainly, from what I understand, they have the best of workmen. It is to be called Troy. Perhaps, when he is a grown man, my grandson, Odysseus, may visit it. . . .'

Afterword

Any pair of authors who have made what they hope is a piece of fresh fiction out of some of the oldest tales in the world, often retold, should perhaps explain why they have done this, and what the relationship is between their work and those tales themselves in their original form or forms.

The desire to write this book sprang out of a conversation in which both of us discovered that, as children, we had been deeply affected by the Greek myths. It seemed to us that from those great stories we had drawn some of our earliest and most powerful impressions of the nature of human destiny, and of the quality and force of human passion. We had not, of course, known that this was happening at the time; but looking back, we could see that part of the great empty map of existence was filled in for us, in a potent and general and deeply influential fashion, by those myths. Here were love and lust; power and powerlessness; cunning and simplicity; anger and despair, and weakness and courage. In no stories that we ever heard were these passions so embodied as in the Greek myths. We could see (so our conversation went) that this must be so because not only were these tales the ancestors of most of the stories that have been written since, but there must cling to them the force and fervour of the intention with which they were invented. This intention was, if not to explain life, then to provide a pattern that would act as a vast imaginative alternative to an explanation. The pattern was designed to embrace and, in this most subtle way, to account for the origin of life; the strength and persistence of the elements as opposed to the frailty and brevity of human existence; the great tangle of human qualities; and that paradox that lies in our power to imagine, and almost at times to become part of, forces both purer and infinitely more lasting than ourselves.

It seemed to us, on the strength of our own remembered experiences as children, quite absurd to regard these myths as mere ancient romances, or agreeable fantasies, or superannuated religious fables. At best (from the point of view at which we had now arrived), those re-tellings that now have most currency among the young form a haphazard sequence of tall tales, often related in a manner which arises from certain conventions of translation from Greek poetry, and have little in them of the literary voice of our own time. We wondered if it might be possible to discover some new style of telling these stories—a language freed in some important respects from those conventions. But more than that—we felt there was room for an attempt to tell the mythical story not as a collection of separate tales but as a continuous narrative. Clearly, with such a rich and disparate range of stories, some early and some late, all of them remoulded again and again, added to and deviously modified by the Greeks themselves as the need grew to account for their more and more complex political and social and religious life—clearly, we could not hope to fit all the pieces together as if they were part of a single jigsaw puzzle: if they had ever been that, in the form in which they survive they resist with the ferocity of Zeus himself any attempt to make continuous sense of them.

But already, before we began writing, we were aware that about the whole body of these myths there flickered a thousand possibilities of coherence: there must be many ways of weaving together a selection from them that would enable whatever story was so composed to carry the whole weight of significance the myth-makers meant their inventions to bear. It would be a matter of so exposing ourselves to these stories that we might begin to sense how, beginning here or there, and moving through the great mythical landscape from this spot to that, we could tell a total tale that, while it would miss out much, in terms of the quantity that is offered, would miss out as little as possible in terms of the entire meaning of the whole mythical structure.

This we did; and we have been deeply moved to discover ourselves borne, by some current starting up within that landscape, on a journey we could not have mapped out before we began writing. We wish to assure readers that it is one journey only among many that we believe possible. Anyone who desires to take his own course might do worse than what we did ourselves—which was to come, after much reading, to a dependence on four books. They are the *Iliad* and the *Odyssey* of Homer (we used E. V. Rieu's fine Penguin translation); the *Metamorphoses* of Ovid; and Robert Graves's *The Greek Myths*, also published by Penguin. Homer gave us the immense size of the stories, the very air of them. Ovid provided us with touches and flashes of colour—and also with many temptations: to all of which we did not succumb, since Ovid was at times a splendid twister of received narrative. We intended to invent, certainly, but not to twist. We were resolved to invent only within the logic of the myths: that is to say, for every turn of every myth we touched on, there is a basis in the most scholarly accounts of them we could find. Which brings us to Mr Graves, to whom our debt is very great. His two volumes are the fruit of a lifetime's study: surely among the most readable source-books in any field. That aim of ours which remained among our first aims—to set down nothing that might be at odds with reputable versions of the myths a young reader might else-where have encountered—was possible to realise largely because we had the work of Mr Graves at our elbows.

We hope we might also have realised part at least of that other aim: to provide such a telling of them as will, for young readers of our time, make them of that order of sources of imagi-native understanding of life that they were for us, long ago. There is no hope that we today can feel of the myths what the Greeks themselves must have felt of them: we cannot call to our aid that degree (and spontaneity and innocence) of belief in Olympus and in the possibility of divine participation in human affairs. But it would be odd if we, and especially the young, had ever lost our power to respond to the magical transformations and the marvellous uncertainty as to what is real that, while it is at the heart of the myths, seems unlikely ever to be far from the heart of man, whatever distance he travels. And what we have ourselves become aware of, as we have worked through our story, is the eternal modernity of the myths. To feel the force of what they have to say about human passions and about the tragedy and comedy and violence and tenderness of the existence of Prometheus's creatures, we do not have to be ancient Greeks. Charles Keeping, when he came to make his own contribution to this book, felt this so strongly that he set out to avoid any suggestion of a definite period: he felt he wanted to rescue the myths from illustration based on Greek vase paintings as we wanted to rescue them from a style based on Victorian translation. He was moved, as we were, by a sense of the enormous violent energy that underlies the myths—by a power so great that, he has said, it would seem a mistake to illustrate particular incidents. A world of immense, dissolving shapes—though it is through very exact and exciting tales that this world, in the myths, makes itself evident, it is in the end with the mysteries of creation and destruction (when, like Sisyphus in the wood near Corinth, we hardly know what we are seeing) that this story is concerned.

LEON GARFIELD

EDWARD BLISHEN